FREEDOM
A N D
RESPONSIBILITY

Christian Science
Healing for Children

Published by
The First Church of Christ, Scientist,
in Boston, Massachusetts, U.S.A.

Acknowledgments

Grateful acknowledgment is made to The Christian Science Publishing Society for permission to reprint articles first published in the *Christian Science Sentinel*, *The Christian Science Journal*, and *The Christian Science Monitor*. Nathan A. Talbot, "The Position of the Christian Science Church," reprinted with permission from *The New England Journal of Medicine*. Lois O'Brien, "Prayer's Not a Gamble," reprinted with permission from author and *U.S. News & World Report*. Jim Meyer, "The Spiritual-Healing Alternative," reprinted with permission from author. Tim MacDonald, "Choosing Spiritual Healing over Medicine," reprinted from *The Boston Globe* with permission from author. "Christian Scientists Care," reprinted with permission of author from *The Press Democrat*. Excerpt from Robert Peel, *Spiritual Healing in a Scientific Age*, reprinted with permission from author and Harper & Row Publishers, Inc. Excerpt from Stephen Gottschalk, "Spiritual Healing and the Law: A Dispute," copyright 1988 by The Christian Century Foundation and reprinted by permission from *The Christian Century*, Oct. 19, 1988. Excerpt from Thomas C. Johnsen, "Christian Scientists and the Medical Profession: A Historical Perspective," reprinted by permission from *Medical Heritage*. David N. Williams, "Christian Science And The Care Of Children: The Constitutional Issues," used with permission from *Church and State*. "Healing: A Christian Science Conviction Raises Serious Legal Questions," reprinted by permission from *The Cincinnati Enquirer*. "Religion: Real or Show?" reprinted by permission from the *Mooresville Tribune*. Dr. Robert Mendelsohn, "Berkeley Researcher Examines Risks of Routine X-Rays," reprinted by permission from Columbia Features, Inc. Eugene D. Robin, M.D., "It Wasn't a Crime but an Error of Judgment," reprinted by permission from author. Letter to the editor in the Santa Rosa *Press Democrat*, reprinted by permission from author and *The Press Democrat*. Janet B. O'Neil, letter to the editor, reprinted by permission from author and *The Florida Times-Union*. Melvin A. Drake, M.D., letter to the editor, reprinted by permission from author. Robert L. McCollom, M.D., letter to the editor, reprinted by permission from author. Stig K. Christiansen, Letter, from *Update: A Quarterly Journal on New Religious Movements*, reprinted with permission from author and The Dialog Center, Aarhus, Denmark. Excerpt from Stephen Gottschalk, "Spiritual Healing on Trial: A Christian Scientist Reports," copyright 1988 by The Christian Century Foundation and reprinted by permission from author and *The Christian Century*, June 22–29, 1988.

Contents

Prefatory Note

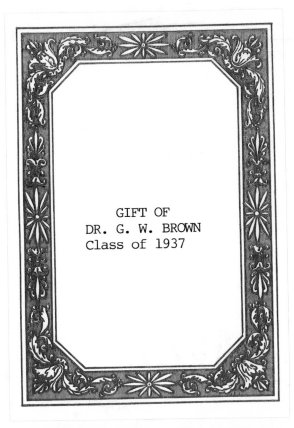

Prefatory note

How do families who practice Christian Science healing care for their children in times of illness?

This question has been much discussed in the media recently. And it has a simple answer. Christian Scientists approach caring for their children just as other parents do: with a deep and natural desire to see their children happy and well. They have, overall, a commendable record in caring for their children's health, as well as a strong record of cooperation with public health officials when questions involving the health of others are involved.

Still, a small number of highly publicized losses of children among Christian Scientists have raised widespread controversy about their approach to healing generally and care for children specifically. There is no evidence or indication that Christian Scientists lose children disproportionately to other groups in the population. Yet since 1984 these losses have resulted in prosecutions of parents, stimulating discussion of related religious, ethical, legal and constitutional issues in newspapers, magazines, and in radio and TV forums. And they have caused much soul-searching among Christian Scientists.

The perspective that dominates discussion of these issues in the media today, reflecting as it does the secular orientation of our society, is largely adverse to Christian Scientists' point of view. As the words "freedom and responsibility" in its title suggest, the following collection is intended to provide the kind of balance on the subject which anyone wishing to arrive at an informed judgment would naturally want to have.

Most of the documents contained herein have been published in other forums. Most, though not all of them, are by Christian Scientists. But they reflect far more than just Christian Scientists' views on controversial questions about their healing practice. They include often-ignored yet indispensable facts about how Christian Scientists approach caring for their children. Without these facts, a rounded assessment of this issue is impossible.

This compilation is organized around four questions which have been central to the debate on this issue:

- What health care do Christian Scientists provide their children?
- What is the evidence for Christian Science healing?
- Should Christian Science healing for children be accommodated in law?
- How would restricting Christian Science healing for children affect society?

Concluding this discussion, there is an appendix containing an empirical study of medical evidence of healings in recent Christian Science periodicals.

This book has been prepared under the supervision of the Manager of Christian Science Committees on Publication. Further copies can be obtained from Christian Science Reading Rooms or

Committee on Publication
The First Church of Christ, Scientist
175 Huntington Avenue
Boston, MA 02115

1

*What health care
do Christian Scientists
provide their children?*

THOSE who know little about Christian Science may be unsure about the care that Christian Science parents provide their children in times of illness. The articles in this section describe the effective care given children in Christian Science families. First, a statement provided upon request by the Church to the Atlanta Centers for Disease Control gives a helpful overall view of this care.

• • •

Statement for Atlanta
Centers for Disease Control

Reprinted in the *Christian Science Sentinel*, September 8, 1986, pp. 1664–1667

FOR more than a hundred years now, Christian Scientists have been practicing a religious teaching which embraces spiritual healing as a natural outcome of understanding and practicing Biblical truths. They maintain a deep love for their families and their children and choose to rely on this method of healing not out of dogmatism but because they have honestly come to feel—often over four and five generations in a family—that it's the most effective way of caring for themselves.

Although this approach is radically different from the practice of conventional medicine, it has its roots in the New Testament approach to healing and the subsequent healing work that developed within the Christian Church. Though Christian Scientists are quite distinct in the way they care for themselves, they are intelligent and informed people. They are farmers and business people, legislators and astronauts, homemakers and physicists—with a reputation for being thoughtful and productive members of society.

Christian Science does not deny that within a strictly physical framework disease can be attributed to physical causes. But it maintains that from a larger, a spiritual perspective, disease is ultimately the result of living within a radically limited view of God and the nature of man. Healing in Christian Science is accomplished through drawing closer to God and experiencing more fully His love. Christian Scientists don't see this as merely an intellectual process but rather a whole way of life involving deep prayer, moral regeneration, and an effort to live in accord with the teachings and spirit of the Bible.

This approach may sound abstract from a purely clinical view, but it has been very concrete in the lives of Christian

3

Scientists. For over a hundred years accounts of healing have been published in church periodicals, though these represent only a fraction of the healings that have occurred in the Christian Science movement. A substantial amount of some fifty thousand published accounts involve medically diagnosed diseases, in many cases determined to be congenital, incurable, or terminal. During a recent ten-year period, over 40 percent of the published testimonies concerning a specific physical disorder involved conditions that had been medically diagnosed. Approximately 10 percent of these healings were confirmed by follow-up examination.

This is not to say that Christian Scientists claim a perfect healing record any more than doctors do. Yet the cumulative evidence of Christian Science healing is such that those who practice this method of care feel it deserves to be judged on its overall record instead of on the basis of isolated failures.

While this approach to healing is substantially different from material medicine, in many ways it is just as different from faith healing. Unlike many in faith healing groups, Christian Scientists are free to choose whatever form of treatment they wish for themselves and their families. While they normally rely on spiritual healing because of its proven effectiveness in their lives, they are under no church compulsion to do so. An individual choosing medical treatment is not abandoned by his church. It's not possible, however, to combine the Christian Science approach to healing with medicine, since they are based on such entirely different premises. To attempt to combine them would be unfair to both methods and to the patient, since it would be pulling him in two different directions.

Christian Scientists do not share the antagonism toward public health officials and doctors that is characteristic of some faith healing groups. While taking a different approach to healing, they feel genuine appreciation for the humanitarian efforts of physicians to relieve suffering. It's in this spirit that Christian Scientists have a long history of cooperation with public health officials—reporting suspected communicable diseases, it has been said, more consistently than many who rely on medical care. They generally request exemptions from vaccinations when the law provides for it, but at the same time they willingly comply with mandatory immunizations, quarantines, and emergency health procedures. Unlike some faith healing groups which have been widely known for childbirth tragedies, Christian Scientists in accord with the law have a physician or duly accredited midwife in attendance at childbirth.

The Christian Science healing ministry is supported by a well-developed structure, unparalleled in any other church involved in healing outside of traditional medicine. Those in need of healing may request specific treatment from a practitioner, an individual who has established a record of healing others and devotes his or her full time to the healing ministry. Christian Science nurses are available to clean and bind wounds as well as care for the physical needs of those relying on Christian Science for healing. There are nearly thirty Christian Science nursing homes and sanatoriums in the United States and Canada where Christian Scientists may receive nonmedical nursing care.

While relying on a method of healing that is basic to their practice of religion, Christian Scientists strive not to ignore the health concerns of others. They work to understand the needs of others and cooperate with them; and they appreciate similar consideration for their approach to healing.

THE second article in this section deals specifically with the assumption that the only alternatives for health care are conventional medical care or no care at all. It is by Nathan A. Talbot, Manager of the Church's Committee on Publication, and was excerpted from an article published in the textbook *Religion in America*, part of a series of opposing viewpoints on significant current social topics.

• • •

From

"Government should not interfere with personal beliefs"

Nathan A. Talbot

Religion in America: Opposing Viewpoints
(San Diego, CA: Greenhaven Press, Inc., 1989), pp. 140–145

PERHAPS the most common stereotype of Christian Scientists is reflected in the comment, "Oh, those are the people who don't go to doctors:" or even "Those are the ones who refuse to give their children medical care." If that's all the information one has to go on, questions like "Do parents have the right to deny their children medical care?" can seem pretty rhetorical. Who doesn't want children to get the care that they need?

The question "Do parents have the right to deny their children medical care?" implies that the only options are medical care or denial of medical care—and that all responsible parents necessarily choose medical care. To ask this question of parents who are known for abusing or neglecting children would be understandable. But to address the same question to responsible, law-abiding parents who obviously love their children, and who have a strong past record of caring for them devotedly and well, is more problematic.

If the only two options for care *were* medical treatment or no treatment, Christian Scientists like others would undoubtedly choose medical treatment. Based on long experience, though, they've found that the choice is not actually limited to those options. For well over a century, Christian Scientists have been relying on spiritual healing for their families—and they've seen extensive healing results, in many instances after medicine could do no more.

Everyone agrees that children need responsible care. In light of Christian Scientists' experience, the real question is: Should parents be obligated to give their children medical care, or is there an alternative way to care for children responsibly?

The word "care" has many connotations. For purposes of this discussion, perhaps we can define "care" or "responsible care" simply as a consistent form of treatment which regularly and effectively meets the needs and maintains the well-being of recipients.

This definition doesn't limit care to medical care alone. But it does distinguish between merely subjective, isolated, or chance success in healing and a more uniform and dependable standard of treatment (e.g., one wouldn't want to generalize that lime jello was a responsible treatment for chicken pox just because one individual appeared to get better after eating it or because one "healer" consistently recommended it!).

Conversely, no matter how logical or scientific a method of treatment appears, it would hardly be a responsible method if the majority of those who received it were not benefited. Nor would it make sense to pan a whole method of treatment as irresponsible because of an occasional loss, however tragic.

For Christian Scientists, reliance on disciplined prayer is a way of life deeply rooted in reason and love—not merely a religious dogma. They see this approach to healing as based on uniform spiritual law governing the whole of life rather than an arbitrary belief in "God's will" for a particular person. Hence Christian Scientists' conviction that spiritual healing can be practiced systematically, even "scientifically," though this practice involves heartfelt devotion to the work of understanding God rather than the usual experimental detachment of a research lab.

Christian Scientists believe that the healings that have been so much a part of their experience aren't random or exclusive. When a Christian Scientist turns to God in prayer, he is not pleading with God to make an exception in his case and heal him. Rather, he is turning more wholeheartedly to God to perceive the underlying spiritual law which rules out illness and inharmony in proportion as it is understood.

Christian Scientists see specific, consistent prayer not merely as a vague help (i.e. like a placebo) but as a definite form of treatment. In trying to understand what such treatment is, it may be helpful to clarify several things it is not. Specifically:

• It is not positive thinking, nor is it based on the belief that healing results from some form of "mind over matter." True prayer involves something much deeper—a heartfelt yielding to God's presence and power.

- It does not ignore illness or injury nor dismiss it blithely as "an illusion." Christian Scientists like other responsible parents love their children far too much to ignore suffering, or the need for comfort and healing.
- It is not a form of "faith healing" or "miracle" in the usual sense of those terms. Nor is blind faith something that Christian Scientists see as particularly helpful in any area of life.
- It is not something forced on people. Christian Scientists deeply respect each person's ability to discern what is right in a given instance. Those who choose Christian Science treatment even in difficult situations are likely to do so—not out of any peer pressure—but because they've found from previous experience that it has effectively and reliably met the need.

Healings through prayer in Christian Science are not a once-in-a-lifetime experience. They are natural everyday occurrences which involve far more than physical healing, however necessary and welcome that is. In fact as one writer put it, "In looking back on a healing, the Christian Scientist is likely to think, not 'That was the time I was healed of pneumonia,' but 'That was the time I learned what real humility is,' or 'That was the time I saw so clearly that all power belongs to God.' "

Perhaps because genuine spiritual healing usually includes a quiet change of heart or understanding, one isn't as likely to hear about [it] on the evening news nor read about [it] in one's local paper or the latest medical journal. But that alone doesn't make the healings any less real. In fact, although some critics try to dismiss the evidence of Christian Science healing as merely "hearsay" or "anecdotal," that kind of labeling seems pretty irrelevant to a father whose young daughter is happily bounding around after being healed of dysentery or the family whose loved ones have been healed of serious injuries sustained in a car accident.

While those uncomfortable with religion or unfamiliar with spiritual healing may feel it has been outmoded by the technological breakthroughs of the past century, Christian Scientists feel that it has an immense contribution to make to the world—and that, far from being outmoded, it is only just beginning to be understood.

THOSE unacquainted with Christian Science and its approach to healing might associate it with what is generally called "faith healing." As both the preceding article and the statement provided to the Atlanta Centers for Disease Control point out, Christian Science differs markedly in a number of ways from the beliefs and practices of fundamentalist faith healing groups that, in recent years, have aroused media attention. These include its overall record of good care for children, Christian Scientists' cooperation with public health officials, and the support system consisting of Christian Science practitioners, nurses, and care facilities available for those seeking spiritual healing.

Christian Science also differs from the older image of "faith healing" generally associated with Pentecostal revival meetings. The following article by David Brooks Andrews, a Christian Scientist who has explored the relation of Christian Science to other forms of spiritual healing, explains how.

• • •

Breaking stereotypes about healing

David Brooks Andrews

SHORTLY after World War II—between 1947 and 1958—
healing revivals flourished, largely independent of organized denominations. Revival tents were pitched. Audiences were drawn by the promise of witnessing or experiencing a miracle. Some revivalists claimed to identify people's illnesses and to know when they were healed. Some experienced electric currents in their hands as they prayed for the sick. Some practiced exorcism of demons. For every style or practice of healing, there was an evangelist who advocated another method. "They tried to develop a common doctrine of healing, but they tolerated great diversity," writes a religious historian of the period.[1]

Before the post-World War II healing revival had lost its momentum, it had done as much to define the term "faith healing" as had Pentecostal evangelists in the early years of this century or television ministers in recent times. Images were popularized that to this day are associated in public thought with almost any effort to turn to God for healing. As a result, it's widely believed that the only way to practice New Testament healing in the 20th century is through mass rallies or some form of faith healing.

Yet during the time the independent healing revivals were winding down, an experience was shared over a Christian Science radio program that illustrates a very different approach to healing. It's an approach that Christian Scientists were practicing long before the healing revivals (or their Pentecostal forerunners) and is an approach that they continue to practice today.

A woman told how she had been healed of cancer—too far advanced for surgery, according to a physician's diagnosis—

through the spiritual deepening and purifying of her life. Her healing involved studying the lives of the disciples, not only their spiritual strengths but the human failings each had to overcome as well. In the process, she discovered the need to face some of the same failings herself.

A Christian Science healing earlier in her life of a congenital heart condition that physicians had pronounced incurable helped to give her courage. She persisted, convinced that, in her own words, "the understanding of the truth and love [Christ Jesus] taught could cleanse my thought of jealousy, doubt, pride, apathy—everything standing in the way of my healing." She went on to say, "It took a number of years, but these were fruitful years. There was a wonderful mental purging going on during that time, and it led to a complete healing." [2]

Of course, many Christian Science healings are quick—some even immediate. Nevertheless, this woman's experience illustrates an important fact about spiritual healing as practiced by Christian Scientists: it involves a person's inner life, particularly his or her relationship to God. In this case, it required facing thoughts, habits, or character traits that would attempt to separate one from God's healing power—allowing the Love that is God to dissolve them. In other words, it required deep Christian repentance and regeneration.

This is not to say that one needs to be eligible for "sainthood" before experiencing physical healing, nor that every healing necessarily involves profound soul-searching on the part of the one needing to be healed. But the overarching fact remains that healing as Christian Scientists understand it is not simply an outward event or exhibition. For them, as for many other Christians today, the process of healing is not something that necessitates or is even benefited by an audience; it doesn't serve as a means to draw crowds or to engage their emotions. Christian Scientists find that the prayer, study, and listening which contribute to healing involve entering into one's closet—into the quiet precincts of prayer—as Jesus taught.

It's not unusual for Christian Scientists to experience physical healing at a church service—as a result of the inspiration and love that are poured into the service—but this happens as quietly as if it had taken place in their own home. Others in the congregation often don't learn of the experience until it is shared during the testimony portion of a Wednesday evening meeting, sometimes weeks later.

Whether at home or in church, a person seeking healing in Christian Science benefits from a supportive mental atmosphere. But the atmosphere that is most supportive of Christian Science healing is remarkably different from the drama and emotions that have come to characterize faith healing revivals. Christian Scientists find that the healing power of the Holy Spirit does not require supernatural signs or a stirring up of emotions in order to bring healing to their lives. Nor does it require forceful, charismatic personalities to intervene with God on behalf of those needing healing. It involves, instead, a whole way of life.

Sometimes when healing's most needed, it can be tempting to feel too exhausted to yield to God or even to think clearly about Him. An editorial published in the *Christian Science Sentinel* several years ago stated: "We don't have to find vigor in a mortal man or circumstance. It isn't there anyway. It was, after all, 'the Spirit of God descending like a dove,' the Holy Ghost, that animated and empowered Christ Jesus. He was empowered from 'on high,' and so are his followers today." [3] Healing has come in the lives of a number of Christian Scientists simply from recognizing that God, Spirit, is making all whole, independent of what the human mind or emotions are able to muster religiously.

In a system that doesn't call for charismatic personalities or revivals, one may wonder what is the role of the "healer." A Christian Science practitioner—one who is committed to the full-time ministry of healing—approaches his or her work from the standpoint that what's most needed is a larger and deeper sense of God. What's needed is to understand God, not through limited human conceptions but through the spiritual sense and intuition that He provides.

The work of the practitioner, then, is to pray and live in a way that makes it possible for others to understand God more clearly, to feel His presence more tangibly. This is not a matter of asserting control over other people's emotions and thoughts but of yielding oneself to God. As the Discoverer and Founder of Christian Science, Mary Baker Eddy, wrote: "That individual is the best healer who asserts himself the least, and thus becomes a transparency for the divine Mind, who is the only physician; the divine Mind is the scientific healer." [4]

The practitioner's work is to recognize and enable others to recognize God's love operating as spiritual law. To understand God's love in terms of divine law does not mean losing a sense of His tenderness or immediacy, nor does it mean that His individuality is reduced to a mere abstraction.

Sometimes it's assumed that spiritual law implies manipulation of God to serve one's personal will—a sad commentary on the way in which human law has come to be regarded—but God simply can't be manipulated. Only as our lives come into accord with spiritual law, beginning with the Commandments, can we experience the promise and blessings of God's law in His way.

The work of the practitioner is not to petition God to intervene and set aright a tragic human life, an ill body, or a decaying physical universe. It's not to provide the right formula of words or thoughts to which God is obligated to respond. Rather, the practitioner's prayer helps make it possible for the patient to awaken to and participate more fully in what God has already created: the spiritual reality that is at hand, which Jesus described as the kingdom of heaven within each of us. As Jesus proved in his healing ministry, it includes all health and wholeness and satisfaction.

One patient's brief description of a practitioner offers a hint of the unselfish and largely unheralded love that's at the heart of spiritual healing: "I can clearly remember the first time she came to see me. It was on a Saturday afternoon after she had closed her busy practitioner's office for the day. There was torrential rain, and the severe winds had blown her umbrella inside out. Still, she had come. From that time on she called on me each weekday after she had closed her office." As a result of the practitioner's prayer over a period of some months, the boy was healed of multiple sclerosis, which had left him completely paralyzed and virtually blind.[5]

Naturally, faith is an element in such prayer—just as it is of any serious effort to practice Christianity (or of any system of healing, even medical). But this faith is not blind trust, nor is it a test of whether one deserves healing. It involves a willing-ness to accept and go forward with what God is revealing in one's life—about Him and the scientific nature of Christianity.

The Science of Christ, or of Christianity, means that God's love and healing power are as dependable now as they were in Jesus' lifetime. And that spiritual healing does not require some special dispensation or unique degree of faith. It's avail-able to all to be learned and practiced.

[1] David Edwin Harrell, Jr., *All Things Are Possible* (Bloomington: Indiana University Press, 1975), p. 26.

[2] *A Century of Christian Science Healing* (Boston: The Christian Science Publishing Society, 1966), pp. 149–151.

[3] Allison W. Phinney, Jr., "Always enough Spirit for us to rise up and live," *Christian Science Sentinel*, April 1, 1985, p. 538.

[4] Mary Baker Eddy, *Miscellaneous Writings* (Boston: The First Church of Christ, Scientist, 1896), p. 59.

[5] *The Christian Science Journal*, March 1987, p. 48.

PERHAPS the greatest barrier to a balanced assessment of how Christian Scientists care for children is a general incomprehension of what is meant by Christian Science treatment and how it can be an effective means of alleviating suffering and disease. One basic explanation is that Christian Scientists view disease as mentally caused, and therefore subject to treatment through spiritual means. This point is made in a passage from an article by Nathan A. Talbot requested by *The New England Journal of Medicine* exploring the difference between Christian Science and medical practice.

• • •

The position of the Christian Science church

Nathan A. Talbot

Reprinted from *The New England Journal of Medicine*
Vol. 309:1641–1644 (December 29, 1983)

CHRISTIAN Scientists are caring and responsible people who love their children and want only the best possible care for them. They would not have relied on Christian Science for healing—sometimes over four and even five generations in the same family—if this healing were only a myth. Yet they approach the subject of healing on the basis of a very different perspective from that of medical practice.

To them it is part of a whole religious way of life and is, in fact, the natural outcome of the theology that underlies it. This theology, Christian Scientists believe, is both biblically based and deeply reasoned. Indeed, they speak of it as "scientific" because they believe its truth has been demonstrated through practical healing experience time and time again. Certainly, Christian Science is leagues apart from faith-healing groups that have aroused current concerns, and its adherents share neither the fundamentalist theology nor the rigidly proscriptive views of medicine characteristic of these groups. They are given neither to blind invoking of "miracles" nor passive submission to sickness as God's will.

Actually, a basic conviction underlying the healing practice of Christian Science is one that some readers of the Journal may share: that disease and physical suffering are in no sense caused or permitted by God, and that since they are profoundly alien to His creative purpose, it is wrong to resign oneself to them and right to challenge them. To the Christian Scientist this conviction is rooted in both the Old and New Testaments. In its fullest implications, such a conviction furnishes the basis on which illness, seen as an aspect of human alienation from God, can be actively confronted and overcome.

Obviously, Christian Scientists are normal people who feel

just as bad as others when they are ill and want just as much to get well. The common misconception that they try to ignore sickness as an "illusion" is based on a confusion of theological and common-sense usages. They certainly do not close their eyes to human pain and suffering, but neither do they accept disease as part of humanity's genuine, God-given being. They believe that human beings are vastly more than biochemical mechanisms, that because they have a direct relationship to God who is Spirit, their true nature—life and health included—must ultimately be found in a day-by-day spiritual discovery of this relationship. The function of the full-time practitioner of Christian Science is not intended to be equivalent to that of a medical doctor, since it consists entirely of heartfelt yet disciplined prayer that brings to a case needing healing a deeper understanding of a person's actual spiritual being as the child of God. This understanding is held to be the crucial factor in dissolving the mental attitude from which all disease ultimately stems.

This does not deny that within a strictly physical framework of causation, certain conclusions are warranted—for example, that many infections have a bacterial origin. And a Christian Scientist would not presume to question the accuracy from a medical standpoint of a competent diagnosis. What a Christian Scientist does question is the physical framework of causation itself. The basic Christian Science "diagnosis" of disease involves the conviction that whatever apparent forms the disease assumes, it is in the last analysis produced by a radically limited and distorted view of the true spiritual nature and capacities of men and women. To take a medical analogy, a Christian Scientist regards all forms of disease as symptomatic of an underlying condition that needs to be healed. This is the healing, or spiritual wholeness, that he or she seeks to effect through prayer.

As the foregoing excerpt explains, Christian Science and medical treatment clearly rest on differing premises. Yet both constitute forms of *treatment* which actively minister to human needs with the intent of relieving suffering and bringing healing. That Christian Science care for children includes treatment in just this sense is pointedly brought out in the following editorial from a Church publication. This editorial also answers the frequently asked question as to why Christian Science and medical care cannot advantageously be combined.

• • •

What is Christian Science treatment?

Allison W. Phinney, Jr.

in the *Christian Science Sentinel,* May 22, 1989

YOU understand that Christian Scientists rely on prayer for healing. But you've also heard something about Christian Science treatment. You wonder how treatment is different from prayer.

Actually, this kind of treatment is a form of prayer. It proceeds from the fact that God is supremely good and that He doesn't create, nor do His laws sustain, disease and evil. A Christian Scientist who is "treating" illness, for example, is making the effort to acknowledge strongly, and as fully as he possibly can, God's all-presence and goodness. Prayer takes a variety of forms—from petition (simply asking God for His help, for example) to using a prayer that has been familiar from childhood—but Christian Science treatment is the persistent application of spiritual truths to a situation in order to bring healing.

According to Christian Science, illness, along with the other discords of life, is, at bottom, the result of the ignorance, fear, or sin of the human mind. The most basic medicine is therefore not the concoction of a drug or highly refined matter but is the divine Mind and its healing influence. As Christian Scientists view it, this understanding of an infinite, present, and totally good God is the means by which Christ Jesus healed. And as Paul encouraged all Christians to do, the Christian Scientist is striving to have that Mind "which was also in Christ Jesus." [1]

The theology of Christian Science emphasizes again and again the necessity for a deep love and thoroughgoing Christianity in order to treat and to heal in this Christianly scientific way. So there is far more to treatment than its just being a

21

different, and perhaps less costly, kind of "New Age" alternative medicine. The person who would treat effectively in accordance with the Science of Christianity must face up to the deep-seated resistance to the allness of God, divine Mind, that seems to be so much a part of believing oneself to be a mortal separated from God. This victory isn't won halfheartedly, and it surely doesn't come all at once.

What gives treatment its capacity to heal is an awakened understanding that God, Spirit or Mind, really is all-powerful good and that the opposite of God isn't substantial. The spiritual and scientific fact is that God has never created anything less than good, and He is holding His loved child in wholeness and health, in His image.

To treat disease or some other circumstance involves yielding thought to what divine Mind is knowing and giving. The medicine of spiritual treatment is the inspiring truth of God's total goodness and power here with us to an extent beyond anything we might have hoped or imagined.

Until someone has experienced the effect of Christian Science treatment, it might seem a little hard to believe. But the accounts of healing in this magazine each week and the more-than-a-century record of healing, beginning with the one-hundred-page chapter of testimony in *Science and Health with Key to the Scriptures* by Mary Baker Eddy and a similar chapter in her *Miscellaneous Writings*, are those of calm, responsible people. Mrs. Eddy, who discovered Christian Science, describes the basis of such healing succinctly when she writes, "Science depicts disease as error, as matter *versus* Mind, and error reversed as subserving the facts of health." [2]

Treatment is always a form of prayer, yet not all prayer would be treatment. During a church service, for example, I would pray for the congregation but would not *treat* them. I would pray for a friend under medical care in the hospital, but would not treat him or her.

The reasoning behind the position is this. Christian Science treatment is expected to bring change for the better to an individual's state of thought for the purpose of healing. It has a strong, definite effect on the person. Therefore it can't be undertaken without the person's knowledge and request.* And just as you wouldn't use two systems of psychology or two different medical treatments for the same problem in one individual because they would interfere with each other, so you wouldn't mix Christian Science treatment with medicine. The intent might be kindly enough, but in the end the effect wouldn't be beneficial.

Over the last hundred years evidence has been accumulating to show that what people believe has an enormous effect on their bodies. Many objective scientific studies, from those on the healing rate after retinal detachment[3] to the placebo effect on stomach functions,[4] to mention just two out of hundreds, have shown that what the human mind thinks, matters a great deal.

Christian Science explains further that not only is this so but that neither sick nor well matter itself is truly substance; it is an extension of human belief and thought. So even when the "cause" of disease is viral or genetic or some other supposedly material mechanism, its basic source is the error of believing that God, Spirit, is less than All. And the healing truth is that God is the great and only real cause in our lives. This is the releasing, liberating realization at the heart of all Christian Science treatment.

---

* As Mary Baker Eddy makes clear in the Christian Science textbook *Science and Health with Key to the Scriptures*, it is not only natural but necessary for parents to pray for children in their care.

---

[1] Phil. 2:5.
[2] *Science and Health*, p. 319.
[3] See Robert B. Reeves, Jr., "Healing and Salvation: Some Research and Its Implications," *Union Theological Seminary Quarterly*, Winter, 1969, pp. 187–197.
[4] See Richard M. Restak, M.D., *The Mind* (Toronto: Bantam Books, 1988), p. 160.

2

What is the evidence for
Christian Science healing?

CHRISTIAN Scientists do not argue that their form of spiritual healing should be accommodated in law on First Amendment grounds alone.* They care every bit as much as others for the health and welfare of children and totally reject the view that they or anyone has a right to sacrifice the well-being of children to the religious principles of parents. Christian Science families normally rely on spiritual means for healing as part of their religion, but not out of rigid dogmatism. They do so because of strong, continuous proof of its effectiveness.

There is substantial evidence backing up their conviction that the power of Spirit heals today as in Biblical times. Much of this evidence is contained in accounts of healing published in Christian Science periodicals over the last century. The appendix to this book contains a detailed, closely-reasoned empirical study of medical evidence in testimonies of healing that have appeared in these periodicals over the two decades from 1968 to 1989. A careful study of this document is recommended for those wishing to satisfy themselves as to the concreteness and validity of this evidence.

At the same time, however, something far larger and more vital than statistical studies (however useful these are for some purposes) animates Christian Scientists' stand on behalf of spiritual healing. That "something" is a deeply-reasoned conviction based on concrete individual experience. As the debate over spiritual healing has escalated, Christian Scientists have had occasion to speak up on behalf of spiritual healing—not just through abstract arguments, but on the basis of healing experiences they have had and witnessed in their own lives. The forums in which they have done so include magazine articles, guest editorials for newspapers, and letters to the editor. This section begins with a sampling of some of these documents.

* A more extensive discussion of First Amendment questions can be found in Section Four.

• • •

Christian Science convictions

J. Thomas Black, Birmingham
in *Detroit Free Press*, November 9, 1983

THE recent ruling by Judge Richard Kaufman in a Wayne County case involving the religious practice of Christian Scientists has prompted wide discussion. The ruling raised important issues of religious freedom and state obligation, but one aspect of the case has received little attention: the reason Christian Scientists take the view of healing that they do. It isn't a matter of simply accepting dogma.

The lawsuit charging the Christian Science Church with negligence was dismissed on constitutional grounds. But there was really more involved than a legal principle, however important. The case differed fundamentally from the recent much-publicized Hamilton case in Tennessee.

For over a century, Christian Scientists have been responsible citizens known for their quiet reliance on spiritual healing. They love their children dearly. They choose this way of healing not only because they see it as a natural part of New Testament Christianity, but also because it has proved outstandingly effective in their lives. Christian Scientists do not use the First Amendment as an excuse for child neglect.

My wife and I, both Christian Scientists, have raised our children in this teaching. Our experience probably has been fairly typical. There have been the usual challenges and joys of parenthood. As with other families, there have been picnics, PTA meetings, baseball games.

As with parents of other faiths, too, there were times of reaching out to God for help and guidance. Christian Scientists are obviously unusual in relying on spiritual healing. But this is actually part of an approach to life that emphasizes spiritual values held by many—responsibility, service, genuine caring.

This church's healing ministry is carried on in the same spirit. It differs in both teaching and practice from localized "faith healing" groups that have been so much in the news. Christian Scientists do not attribute sickness or death to God's will. They see Christian healing as far more than blindly invoking "miracles."

In fact, healing has been a normal occurrence in Christian Science families over the years. We've seen in our own family healings of the effect of concussion, impetigo, and strep throat, among many others. Friends have been healed of polio and cancer. I mention such experiences only because they are similar to countless others—often medically documented— involving serious as well as everyday problems. This may help readers understand Christian Scientists' convictions about the practicality of Christian healing.

In other words, Christian Scientists turn to such healing because of what they've actually seen of its results through the thick and thin of rearing families over several generations. They make their own free choices. The church does not presume to tell them what they "must" or "must not" do, though it always counsels respect for the law.

What, then, of the tragic case in Wayne County? One mourns with all one's humanity the loss of a child—in or out of a hospital. But even while one feels deeply such a loss, there is an additional perspective that needs to be considered— as everyone recognizes naturally when children die under medical care through complications, misdiagnoses, side effects of drugs, etc., even in normally treatable cases. Reason dictates that Christian Scientists' way of living and healing also be judged by its overall record, not on the basis of a case as unrepresentative as the one in question.

It may be difficult for many in our medically-oriented society to understand this perspective. But it grows out of the experience of those who have seen their children healed again and again through Christian prayer—in some cases after all medical hopes were exhausted. Our church could not have lasted for so long as a worldwide denomination if its overall record were not very good indeed.

Is society really at the point where this kind of conscientious faith and experience is simply to be dismissed? This was the underlying issue in Wayne County.

Christian Scientists recognize the profound responsibility that goes along with this question. They feel as strongly as others that religious freedom should not become a loophole for cases in which mistreatment and neglect actually do occur. They raise these concerns earnestly, mindful of Christ's unfailing compassion for the "little ones" in his midst.

Prayer's not a gamble

Lois O'Brien

in "Rostrum," *U.S. News & World Report,* April 28, 1986

I'M a concerned grandmother—concerned about the way the media cover criminal prosecutions in my state, California.

Several parents, who are Christian Scientists, have been charged with murder and manslaughter for turning to spiritual healing instead of seeking medical aid for a child who died.

I can't speak for the parents, but as a Christian Scientist I know how much they loved these children. And I know they are not criminals any more than the many equally loving parents who have had a child die under medical care.

My own family has relied on Christian Science healing for four generations. I have never considered prayer a gamble. Please understand: I'm not speaking of some crude kind of "faith healing" that implores God to heal and says it was His will if nothing happens. I'm speaking of responsible spiritual healing practiced now over a century—by many perfectly normal citizens and caring parents.

I'm concerned about not being taken seriously—that nobody in the media (and this includes *U.S. News & World Report*) is really taking into account that these healings have been happening over many years. Not just in my family, not just my friends. I'm speaking of the massive, long-term experience in a whole denomination.

These healings just don't seem to register. Again and again, articles are written as if they had never occurred. It seems as if a portion of our society just can't stand to have its "enlightened" secular assumptions questioned by seriously considering the evidence of Christian healing in our time.

Christians in many denominations are taking spiritual healing more and more seriously. Why then should it be dismissed in the media and in the framing of public policy?

In a country founded on a quest for religious freedom, there needs to be room for differences—even major ones. This is not to say that religious freedom gives anyone the right to neglect or mistreat their children. Or that Christian Scientists any more than others should be given a blank ticket. But where there is a caring home environment and a track record of healing in many thousands of families, the law should not take away the choices of those who love these precious children most. Nor should the media ignore the overwhelming record of good care they have been given.

Lois O'Brien lives in Davis, California, where she taught rhetoric for many years at the University of California.

The spiritual-healing alternative

James H. Meyer

in *The Denver Post*, June 21, 1986

IMPORTANT issues are coming to the fore relating to people's rights and responsibilities in caring for themselves and their families.

Just recently, the Supreme Court invalidated federal regulations requiring life-prolonging medical treatment for severely handicapped "Baby Doe" infants. This decision gives those closest to these heart-rending situations the right to decide what's best without undue government interference.

In another instance, two Western Slope men turned to their fundamentalist faith for healing after being burned in a natural gas explosion. Their choice stirred understandably deep emotions, ranging from condemnation to grudging respect for the pair's courage to sadness when one of the men died.

A Post editorial written in the aftermath of this incident (May 11) raised another topic—the legal obligations of parents who rely on religious healing to care for their children. Genuine love and understanding are greatly needed in sorting this issue through.

As a Christian Scientist, I can't pretend to speak for others, but I can offer a perspective on why people of my own non-fundamentalist, but nevertheless Christian, faith feel so deeply about spiritual healing as they've practiced it for the past century.

I've avoided the term "faith healing" because in the usual sense it doesn't really fit Christian Scientists. They approach spiritual healing as a systematic study and practice. It isn't a hit-or-miss thing, but a way of life much as the Quakers' witness for peace is a way of life.

Christian Scientists see God's love as the healing power, and understanding prayer rooted in this love as having a dimension beyond merely "asking for a miracle." They reject the attitude that it's divine will if a person isn't healed.

A support network is available to aid the healing process. This includes Christian Science practitioners—individuals who devote their full-time to the healing ministry—Christian Science nurses, and non-medical care facilities. As an article on the practitioner's role in the Journal of Pastoral Counseling has stated, healing in Christian Science is understood as involving not only physical ills, but the whole spectrum of human discords.

Christian Scientists see true spiritual healing not as a dogma, but as a rational choice. This choice is natural to those who've witnessed numerous examples of God's healing power over the years.

Current laws relating to religious healing reflect this long experience. One particular provision in the Colorado Children's Code, however, has come under criticism recently as local faith-healing groups have sprung up in increasing numbers.

The provision states that a child "under treatment by . . . spiritual means" rather than conventional medicine isn't considered neglected "for that reason alone." This doesn't mean "anything goes" just because it's done in the name of religion. But it signals the legislature's intention not to make reliance on spiritual healing automatically a crime.

The provision was written to apply only to the practice of healing in a "recognized church or religious denomination"—a wording questioned in the recent Post editorial because of the difficulty of defining that phrase precisely. In the context of the statute, it implies at least an organized system of spiritual healing with reasonable successful results. The wording was intended to protect children from erratic religious practices without closing the door on responsible spiritual healing.

When the provision was passed in its present form some 20 years ago, Christian Scientists had been practicing spiritual healing consistently for decades. Their responsibilities and rights as parents had long been broadly established in the law.

As far back as 1899, the governor of this state had vetoed a medical society bill that would have prohibited such healing—a veto which the Post supported.

Over the several generations since then, literally hundreds of thousands of children have been raised in this country under Christian Science care. There is no evidence that these children have been any less healthy as a group than other children, or that fewer of them have survived to healthy adulthood. This, more than any other factor, explains the relatively tolerant legal climate toward spiritual healing that evolved not only in Colorado but in the nation.

The state has a vital role in protecting children, but it shouldn't take away choices of responsible and loving parents where this kind of healing record exists. What's best for children can't always be reduced to imposing medical treatment on them. Nor can the legal issues honestly be approached as if real healings haven't happened in Christian Science families, or as if they were rare exceptions.

My own father was healed in Christian Science after kind and dedicated physicians were honest enough to say they could offer him no lasting cure. Because of his healing, my parents became Christian Scientists. In raising my own family, we've continued to turn to Christian Science for healing. It's been very reliable in meeting our needs.

Increasingly, sincere people of different religious persuasions are coming to feel that spiritual healing has a place in today's world. Certainly, the subject of Christian healing needs to be approached humbly, with an awareness of how much there is to learn. But in view of society's enormous needs, public officials should be slow to restrict the freedom of conscientious people to practice spiritual healing.

James H. Meyer is the Christian Science Committee on Publication for Colorado.

Choosing spiritual
healing over medicine

Timothy A. MacDonald
in *The Boston Globe*, June 5, 1988

F OR more than a century, Boston has been the headquarters of the Christian Science Church. We hope our neighbors know us well enough by now to recognize that we aren't religious fanatics—that we take seriously our responsibility to our families and community.

Manslaughter charges were recently filed in the Suffolk County Superior Court in a case involving the death of a child under Christian Science care. News reports have tended to center on two questions: Were the parents "recklessly neglectful" in seeking help for their child in the healing practice of Christian Science instead of turning to medicine? Is it appropriate for the law to recognize serious spiritual healing as a legitimate form of care in responsible families? Christian Scientists have practiced such healing legally here and throughout the country for many decades.

As a Christian Scientist and parent, I have found myself doing much soul-searching during the past weeks: "What would I do if I had been in this family's position?" "Am I recklessly stubborn in my reliance on God?" "Why have I elected to rely on spiritual means for healing instead of medical care?" I would like to share some thoughts that have come to me.

When my wife and I had children, we faced decisions all parents face on how to care properly for children. It was during those years that we began the serious study of Christian Science.

No parents who deeply love their children want them to suffer in any way. Whenever either child was sick, we had to decide what healing approach was best for the child at that time—not what was easiest for us, certainly not putting so-called church doctrine ahead of a child's life, but what was going to meet the child's needs.

In some early instances when we didn't feel confident of meeting the need spiritually, we turned to medical help. But as our spiritual study deepened, we saw more and more evidence of the healing power of reasoned prayer. There were significant physical healings. It wasn't a matter of blind faith or the "power of the mind," but of prayer becoming a way of life, rooted in the conviction that a loving God couldn't also be the cause of sickness or suffering. The doctor visits no longer seemed the best way to go. We felt we'd found a basis for trusting something deeper—more demanding, but ultimately more reliable.

I don't think one can imagine secondhand a parent's feelings in losing a child. But I do know that Christian Scientists aren't neglectful in the care they give or the way they approach decisions. My wife and I took the care of our children seriously, and one of the factors we had to face when they were sick was that medicine doesn't have all the answers . . . .

Placing our children under medical care might have been legally safer for us as parents, but we wanted what was best and safest for the children. And it was a decision only we could make; it wasn't a decision based on hindsight, but on our best judgment at the moment.

If Christian Scientists felt that the conscientious practice of spiritual healing resulted in more "preventable" deaths than occur routinely under medical care, they would be more inclined to turn to medical care. However, such deaths haven't been even remotely close to normal in their experience. That is the main reason Christian Scientists' healing practice has for so long been permitted under law.

The healing that has gone on in Christian Science families for so many years—often medically documented, rarely reported in the press—means every bit as much to those families as the healing that has gone on in hospitals means to others. The choice of spiritual healing in this context is not frivolous, but based on the experience of restored health in literally hundreds of thousands of cases ranging from minor to life-threatening.

No one denies the need to protect children carefully and humanely in a society that often seems hostile to the very idea of childhood. The power of the courts to intervene in extreme cases is already legally established. No one is saying anything as simplistic and indefensible as "religious freedom is more important than children's lives," or that "there should be no limits to parental autonomy."

What we are saying is that the significant successes of Christian Science healing cannot be overlooked. That something more needs to be considered than a tragic set of circumstances with accompanying tragic headlines.

Timothy A. MacDonald is a Christian Science practitioner and teacher and a former First Reader of The Mother Church in Boston.

Christian Scientists care

"Another View," *The Press Democrat*, Santa Rosa, California, July 22, 1989

As I've read the papers, I've wondered whether my neighbors are having as much difficulty as I am reconciling the rather bizarre descriptions of Christian Scientists given in the newspaper with the actual Christian Scientists they've known as neighbors, colleagues and friends.

There's no question that the beliefs and practices of Christian Scientists differ in some ways from those of our neighbors. And yet, it never seemed to me that differences alone are grounds to judge another a criminal or a member of a cult. In fact, for a good many of us those very differences have become a source of strength and healing for ourselves and our families.

Yes, I know about the several court cases involving children who have died while receiving Christian Science care. These losses are not any easier to bear than the passing of any much-loved child. Like you, I mourn with the parents, the families and all those involved. And along with fellow church members, I've done some soul-searching—and some recollecting, too.

Nearly 50 years ago, as a widow with three young children to raise and support, I had a teenager who hadn't recovered from his bout with polio 10 years earlier. He had received extensive medical care. But his spine was still curved, his head pulled to one side, and he had difficulty coordinating his arms and legs.

Over the next several years, as we turned wholeheartedly to God (and began to rely radically on Christian Science), the child was healed. So completely, in fact, that an Army Air Corps exam several years later found this by now 6-foot, 3-inch young man fit for duty without even a trace of the problem.

I don't know what my neighbors at the time thought of that particular healing or of my new religion. They were not easy years for any of us, and I didn't say much. But from time to time neighbors would call when one of their children was sick and ask me to pray for him or her in Christian Science. The children were healed. Sometimes the parents would ask more about God or Christian Science, sometimes they wouldn't. Some began to study Christian Science for themselves. Many (including some of my own children) did not.

Whether to adopt Christian Science or another teaching as their religion and way of life was up to each of them. In a society like ours, one is constantly being exposed to alternative beliefs and practices. Like many others, I initially turned to Christian Science out of the need to find healing for my son and strength to raise my young family. And, like countless others before and after me, I've continued to rely on it, not out of any coercion, blind faith or ignorance of the alternatives, but naturally—based on my own experience of God and His healing and strengthening presence in raising our family.

From time to time individuals have asked me why, when a child isn't getting better, parents might stick with Christian Science treatment rather than giving the child antibiotics or other medical treatment. Certainly a deep concern for the child may prompt this question—a concern Christian Scientists share. But it's also helpful to stop and think for a moment about how healing actually occurs, whether under medicine or Christian Science care.

In some cases, recovery is quick, in others through slow but steady progress. There also are times when full recovery comes after a condition initially has grown worse or reached a period of crisis. In my own experience as a Christian Scientist, it has been through such healings that I've come to understand a little more of what Jesus meant in saying, "With God all things are possible."

For Christian Scientists who have had similar healings, it may seem very natural and reasonable in tough situations to continue relying on God rather than turning to medical care, with the expectation born of experience that their child, too, will be healed. However, if at any point a couple really felt that another form of treatment might help their child more, I would understand if these same parents—whether Christian Scientists or others—changed to that treatment.

I've always tried in lending a hand to my neighbors to respect their approach to religion and child care. And I've been grateful when they've been willing to do the same.

Over the 40 years I've been a Christian Science practitioner, that kind of growing mutual respect and support has meant a great deal. In that time I've seen a good many children grow up and raise children and grandchildren of their own. At close quarters, it's harder to miss all that we share—our common love and concern for families and their well-being, a common love for God, a respect for law and for the rights of others.

Being neighbors does bring perspective, and, I trust, a willingness to hold off judgment until one actually knows more of what those in our community—including those [who] might not live next door—actually believe and how they actually care for their children.

CHRISTIAN Scientists rest their case for legislative accommodation of their form of healing on the fact that such healing actually *occurs*. It has been said both by Christian Scientists and their opponents that the current debate has had one healthy outcome: it has brought into sharper public focus the question of whether spiritual healing can actually *happen* on a disciplined, consistent basis.

One book that critically examines the question of the evidence for spiritual healing is Robert Peel's path-breaking *Spiritual Healing in a Scientific Age*, published by Harper & Row in 1987. One of the key questions addressed in this book is why there is so much entrenched resistance to serious consideration of the plentiful evidence for spiritual healing. As Peel notes, this resistance has taken several forms, including the tendency to dismiss indisputable spiritual healings as merely "spontaneous remission" or to write off thoroughly attested evidence as merely "anecdotal"—meaning "any account of a healing that has not been under clinical observation from beginning to end" (p. 36).

The following passage from the book, however, relates to a deeper question. It underscores the limitations, in the light of advancing scientific knowledge, of an *a priori* scientism that refuses to consider seriously the evidence for spiritual healing.

. . .

From

"Healing the Sick: Science or Art?"

Robert Peel

Spiritual Healing in a Scientific Age
(San Francisco: Harper & Row, 1987), pp. 22–29

ODAY'S biomedicine rests philosophically on the concept of
the human being as a physical organism shaped in the last
analysis by the interaction of change and law through eons of
cosmic, molecular, geological, and finally biological development. Most professing Christians, including Christian doctors,
would add to that description their own personal faith in a
divine purpose somehow or other at work through this long
evolutionary process. But the fact remains that medicine *as a
putative natural science* must treat the body as a wholly material phenomenon.

By the strict standards of the "hard" physical sciences, the
scientific doctor is the specialist who treats a particular disease,
not the general practitioner who may to some extent minister
to the whole person. The latter may take into account psycho-
logical, social, moral, or even spiritual factors far more important to healing in a given instance than the biochemical
expertise of specialists treating the affected organs or functions
as somewhat autonomous though closely interrelated parts of a
complex material mechanism. Yet the specialists tend to have
the final say in our technological society, with computerized
medicine on hand to produce its statistical data, make its light-
ning diagnoses, and deliver its mechanical judgments—in the
doctor's office, the clinic, the operating room, the emergency
room, the intensive care unit.

The medical triumphs of this century are generally regarded
as among the wonders of our age. Less well known is the
extensive, documented literature challenging modern medicine's right to be accounted an exact science or even a socially
satisfactory system of health care. This dissatisfaction is by no
means confined to such crusading critics as Ivan Illich and

Robert S. Mendelsohn, with their insistence that medical science still causes as many diseases as it cures.[1] The criticisms extend through hundreds of sober medical reports, sociological studies, ethical disquisitions, economic analyses, legal decisions, popular magazine articles, and academic investigations. As President Derek Bok of Harvard ruefully suggested in a carefully balanced 1983 report on the needs of the university's medical school, "Dean Burwell was only partly facetious in stating to Harvard medical students: 'Half of what we have taught you is wrong. Unfortunately we do not know which half.' "[2]

Some physicians believe that the uncertainties of present-day medicine can be cured by a more profound knowledge of biology, the science that underlies today's chemotherapy. But with all the brilliance of its achievements, the molecular biology of our age lags behind quantum physics in recognizing the inherent limits of its own possible knowledge. It is conceivable—indeed, to the Christian it should surely be regarded as inevitable—that in seeking to find the ultimate source of human intelligence in the electrochemistry of the brain and the basic determinant of human character in the molecular architecture of DNA, biology may or must encounter its own revolutionary principle of uncertainty.

Twenty-five years ago, the perceptive medical biologist René Dubos punctured the widely held thesis that "scientific medicine" was responsible for wiping out or diminishing such great scourges as typhus, scarlet fever, yellow fever, and diphtheria. Rather, he pointed out, the improvement resulted largely from the great humanitarian social reforms of the nineteenth century, which rapidly evolved into public health practices that brought about spectacular improvements in the sanitary and nutritional state of the Western world. This achievement, he wrote, "cannot be credited to the type of laboratory science with which we are familiar today." Instead, it was "the expression of an attitude which is almost completely foreign to the modern laboratory scientist." And he concluded,

Exact sciences give correct answers to certain aspects of life problems, but very incomplete answers. It is important of course to-count and measure what is countable and measurable, but the most precious values in human life are aspirations which laboratory experiments cannot yet reproduce. As Haeckel pointed out, Richtigkeit—correctness—is not sufficient to reach Wahrheit—the real truth.[3]

In tomorrow's world the "real truth" may be very different from the view still holding that human beings are basically physical. In penetrating to such a reality, love may be a more exact instrument than chemical analysis or genetic experimentation, as Dubos recognized.

Even the present scientific world picture holds faint indications of this fact, and more can be expected. Meanwhile, the Christian healing that draws power from deep wellsprings of spiritual perception has a vital part to play in bringing forth that larger science of which Erwin Schrödinger—one of this century's great physicists—could write: "We must be prepared to find a new type of physical law prevailing in it. Or are we to term it a non-physical, not to say a super-physical law?" [4] The Christian has the right to ask: Are we prepared to find that the ultimate science of healing is one with the ultimate art of living—a living out from the divine Spirit or infinite Love we call God?

A wonderful universe may well contain many spiritual wonders unexplainable by current scientific theories. The great surprises lie beyond the piecemeal reductionist empiricism posited on a mechanistic universe. The holistic medicine of today is at least a gesture in that direction, but it falls far short of the challenge offered by Christian healing that relies *wholly* on spiritual means.

What may be our greatest need in this area of experience is a leap of thought to a level of reality beyond the reach of our present scientific instrumentation. This reality is observable and measurable only through its effects on human lives, but even then it does not lend itself to controlled experiment or laboratory analysis.

Wolfgang Pauli who was one of the most prophetic of the remarkable constellation of quantum scientists in the first half of the century made a statement that indicates just such a leap of thought.

> Since the discovery of the elementary quantum, physics was obliged to renounce its proud claim to be able to understand in principle the *whole* of the world. But this predicament may contain the seed of further developments which will correct the previous one-sided orientation and will move towards a unitary world-view in which *science is only a part in the whole.*[5]

This kind of open-ended thinking stands in welcome contrast to the scientific dogmatism that arrogantly rules out, on a priori grounds, the very possibility of such a phenomenon as spiritual healing. Pauli at least leaves the door ajar.

[1] Ivan Illich, *Medical Nemesis* (New York: Pantheon Books, 1976); Robert S. Mendelsohn, *Confessions of a Medical Heretic* (Chicago: Contemporary Books, 1979).
[2] Derek Bok, "Needed: A New Way to Train Doctors," President's Report to the Harvard Board of Overseers, 1982-83, *Harvard Magazine* (May–June 1984), p. 41.
[3] René Dubos, *Mirage of Health* (New York: Harper & Bros., 1959), pp. 17, 234.
[4] Erwin Schrödinger, *What Is Life?* (Cambridge: Cambridge University Press, 1946), p. 86.
[5] Quoted in Arthur Koestler, *The Roots of Coincidence* (London: Hutchinson, 1972), p. 90. Emphasis added.

OVER half of *Spiritual Healing in a Scientific Age* is composed of affidavits of physical healing supplied by direct participants in healing experiences. These accounts, almost all of them by practicing Christian Scientists, cover a wide range of medically diagnosed cases, including broken bones and diseases considered degenerative, incurable, or terminal.

As a review in *The Christian Science Monitor* (August 6, 1987) acknowledged, the book's author honestly came to grips with the fact that spiritual healing occurs in a verifiable life-context, so that it does not fit the model of a fully worked-up case history demanded by those who believe medicine to have reached the status of an exact science.

A review of the book from just such a critic brought forth a letter of rebuttal from Roy Adler, then Committee on Publication for New York, in the newspaper that had run the initial response. The letter, printed in abridgment by the newspaper, follows here in its full form.

• • •

To the editor

Roy Adler

THE Gospel of John tells of a man blind from birth who, after being healed by Jesus, was intensely questioned by those seeking to explain the healing away. First they denied that he had ever been blind; then, when his parents confirmed the fact of the healing, they told him that it couldn't have come through "a sinner" like Jesus. Students of the New Testament may recall the man's honest answer, for which he was cast out of the temple: "Whether he be a sinner or no, I know not: one thing I know, that, whereas I was blind, now I see" (John 9:25).

As a Christian Scientist, I couldn't help but think of those words after reading the recent column " 'Spiritual Healing' Claims Wither on the Vine of Investigation." The column, sharply critical of what it termed "fallacious healing claims," was a rebuttal to an earlier review of Robert Peel's book *Spiritual Healing in a Scientific Age* (Harper & Row, 1987). The original review had termed the book "a cogent and scholarly presentation" of the case for spiritual healing as it has been practiced in Christian Science for many years.

In my own life, I've been so deeply blessed by this practice that it would also be less than honest for *me* to deny the healings I've seen and experienced or to attribute them to a source other than God's grace. Without turning this letter into a personal testimony, a firsthand perspective on the questions raised in the rebuttal column may be helpful to [your] readers in the spirit of the account in John.

Christian Scientists don't expect others simply to "take our word for it" on the reality of spiritual healing, but we do ask that serious evidence of healing be taken seriously. Skepticism is understandable, but fairness is essential. No one denies the need in today's world to ask hard questions about the credibil-

47

ity, accuracy, and medical significance of the evidence. Too often, however, this evidence is approached with the attitude, "I don't believe in (or don't approve of) such healing, therefore such evidence can't be true."

The experiences of healing related in the Peel book are not merely subjective "claims." However one may explain them, the *fact* of healing in these cases is inescapable. They *happened*. Many are attested by sworn affidavits and all involved conditions that had been medically diagnosed. The range of these conditions includes life-impairing (e.g. blindness and near blindness) as well as life-threatening (e.g. spinal meningitis, cancer).

In none of these cases was the diagnosis casual or tentative. Special care was taken to report the statements of physicians accurately and without exaggeration or misunderstanding. One of the physicians mentioned in the book read the entire manuscript before publication specifically to raise "hard questions" of this kind and exclude cases where it seemed possible that a patient may have misconstrued a doctor's words. In one case where such questions were raised, for example, the testifier obtained (with some difficulty because of hospital policy) extensive medical records documenting the serious heart condition of which she was healed in Christian Science.

Because of the sensitive nature of its subject, the book omits doctors' names in reprinting many of the affidavits. Nevertheless, numerous names of doctors and hospitals *are* given, and the individuals testifying to healings are identified. Thus, these healings are not merely "church" assertions. They are recounted by the people who actually experienced them, moved by deep and understandable gratitude for what happened. They involve life situations with all the complexities, medical and otherwise, that real life brings. What they have in common is that they are all experiences in which profound Christian prayer and inner regeneration has cut through these complexities with tangible outward effect.

The Peel book does not pretend that individual case evidence automatically answers all medical or scientific questions about spiritual healing. But this evidence has accumulated in the lives of at least several hundred thousand practicing

Christian Scientists over the past several generations, and it is too massive to be dismissed simply on the ground that it does not take the form of statistics from controlled studies. While true prayer isn't something that can readily be tested "experimentally" in the same manner that medicines or drugs are tested, that's no excuse for arbitrarily ruling out the evidence that does exist in other forms.

The writer of the rebuttal column, Rita Swan, argues that orthodox medical care alone protects children and should be forced on everyone. Christian Scientists naturally have a different perspective, reflecting our own long *experience* both as individuals and as a denomination with the practice of spiritual healing. We do not wish to whitewash this experience, to minimize cases when healing hasn't come (any more than good doctors minimize failings in the practice of medicine). But there is so much more to it than the court cases cited by Mrs. Swan—more loving and caring as well as more healing.

The ultimate issue at stake in those court cases goes beyond one denomination's religious practices. A society which limits God's love and power to the margins of the healing process is in danger of losing the deepest source of healing in human lives.

P ERHAPS the most frequent criticism of those who dispute the evidence of spiritual healing is that it is merely "anecdotal" and therefore of negligible significance. This argument was reiterated in two strong criticisms of an article entitled "Spiritual Healing on Trial: A Christian Scientist Reports" by historian Stephen Gottschalk, which had been published in *The Christian Century* (June 22–29, 1988). The criticisms were written by Rita Swan and the Rev. Robert L. Rafford. The same issue that published these letters also included a closely reasoned rejoinder pointing out the fallacies involved in the dismissal of the evidence of spiritual healing as "merely" anecdotal.

• • •

From

"Spiritual Healing and the Law: A Dispute"

Stephen Gottschalk
in *The Christian Century*, October 19, 1988

CHRISTIAN Scientists believe that spiritual healing can be practiced on an intelligible basis. Is it too much to ask that such healing be intelligently assessed? Of course, such healing goes on in the real circumstances of daily life rather than in a laboratory context. By its nature the evidence for spiritual healing does not take the form of statistics flowing from controlled scientific experiments. But this does not mean that no evidence exists. Not every phenomenon must be drawn into the vortex of a rigid scientism before it can be rationally examined.

Rafford bemoans the lack of evidence for an overall assessment of Christian Science healing, while holding to evidential standards so narrow they exclude serious examination of existing evidence. In *Healing Miracles: A Doctor Investigates*, British physician Rex Gardner adopts a more realistic definition of "anecdotal" as a "derisory adjective applied to any case-history that is used to support an argument with which the listener does not agree." Even by Rafford's own definition this evidence cannot be written off as "anecdotal." There is nothing "isolated" about the thousands of healings of specific, diagnosed diseases reported in church periodicals over the years. Nor can they be categorically written off as "unproven" when well over 30 percent of published testimonies involve cases where there has been such a diagnosis or a follow-up examination.

Such accounts are meaningless only if one posits that the testifiers were liars or fools. For example, Swan contemptuously writes off the healing of a boy with a collapsed lung due to pneumonia. But the boy's own firsthand account tells of his family's terror when his condition was diagnosed by X-ray at the hospital, the spiritual experience that led to healing just before surgery was scheduled to take place and the incredulous physician's insistence on taking another set of X-rays, which confirmed that the condition had been healed.

Not only does intellectual integrity require that we assess such experiences in their own terms, but the body of accessible, firsthand testimony of Christian Science healing is probably larger than that of any other nonmedical form of healing. Failures occur and they can be devastating. But it doesn't take a 100 percent success rate in spiritual healing to puncture the assumption that such healing can't happen and to reveal its inadequacy to guide social policy.

Medical practice itself could hardly survive the kind of scrutiny we are told Christian Science healing must come under if its practice for children is not to be legally proscribed. Medical studies show that there are 66,000 fatalities per year in the United States just among children between two and four years of age. Statistics like this should caution us against ignoring the tragic facts and embracing a medical triumphalism unsustained by thoughtful medical opinion. As Eugene D. Robin of Stanford University Medical School has commented, "The present trend of prosecuting Christian Scientists in medically dubious cases poses a threat to medicine. Suppose every physician who committed an error in judgment were brought to trial?"

Given the mixed record of medical practice, the plentiful evidence for the effectiveness of spiritual healing and the slight number of fatalities among children treated through Christian Science (considering that every one is brought to public attention), it is not irrational to say that constitutional protection of free exercise of religion warrants legal recognition of Christian Science care for children.

3

*Should Christian Science
healing for children
be accommodated in law?*

THE ethical and constitutional questions surrounding the issue of legal accommodation of Christian Science healing for children have been widely discussed in the media in recent months. Yet they are not new. On the contrary, legislative recognition of Christian Science healing has a long history, going back to the early days of this century. The primary fact in this history has been the merited recognition by the public generally and legislators specifically of Christian Scientists as responsible citizens, good neighbors, and—most important—caring parents. An article entitled "Christian Scientists and the Medical Profession: A Historical Perspective" by Thomas C. Johnsen in the magazine *Medical Heritage* includes valuable background about legal recognition of Christian Science in earlier decades.

• • •

From

"Christian Scientists and the Medical Profession: A Historical Perspective"

Thomas C. Johnsen

Medical Heritage, January/February 1986

THE American tradition of tolerance worked in [Christian Science's] behalf—and continues to do so—because of what a New York newspaper called the "cumulative" experience of the movement in its healing practice.[1] Many nonadherents who had witnessed healings of Christian Scientists in their own communities spoke out strongly against restrictive measures—in 1903 in Eddy's native New Hampshire, a bill outlawing the practice of Christian Science by name was voted down overwhelmingly even "before the Christian Scientists of the state had time to oppose it."[2]

The issue was rarely settled so quickly in states where Christian Science was less familiar. Nevertheless, nearly every state legislature in the country had specifically rejected proscriptive proposals, sometimes on three or four occasions, by the decade after Eddy's death in 1910. In the few states where such measures were initially passed, governors actually vetoed them or they were revised in subsequent legislative sessions. In the wake of the court cases brought against Christian Science under medical licensing laws, many states incorporated explicit "saving" clauses into their codes affirming the legality of the practice of spiritual healing.

From the Christian Scientists' standpoint, such recognition was a matter of equitable treatment under the law, not of preferential legislation. As former Iowa Judge Clifford Smith explained in 1914, in *Christian Science: Its Legal Status,* they did not seek any "special privilege" or legal establishment of religion, but solely to preserve rights threatened by efforts to prohibit their system of healing.[3] The Smith book, probably the denomination's most thorough articulation of its position, was subtitled *A Defense of Human Rights*; the fact that the subtitle did not include the term "religious rights" was significant, since Christian Scientists saw the issue under consideration as far more than a narrow Constitutional question, or even than merely one of religious freedom. Judge Smith acknowledged, in any case, that such freedom is not absolute, and that it involves not only rights but also responsibilities—what Christian Scientists could properly expect from society and what society could reasonably demand from them.

Christian Scientists saw due regard for public health as a responsibility. In 1901 Eddy herself issued a statement instructing church members to diligently obey legal requirements on vaccination and reporting of suspected contagious conditions—citing Jesus' injunction to "render unto Caesar what is Caesar's." [4] While the *Journal of the American Medical Association* pronounced this statement an implicit "confession" of the failure of Christian Science, her student Alfred Farlow pointed out that it was consistent with the broad emphasis of her teaching of respect for the rights of others: "I readily concede that Christian Scientists must not attempt to set aside the laws which stand for the general good of any community." Farlow admitted that "there may be unwise and careless Christian Scientists, who do and say unwise things," but insisted that "such people would be unwise and careless" whatever church they belonged to and could not be taken as representative.[5] In practice, the group's record of cooperation with public health authorities over many years has borne out the latter assertion.[6]

The most difficult issues of responsibility then, as now, involved the care of children. Christian Scientists could understand the "honest opinion" of doctors on the necessity for medical treatment—most having earlier shared this opinion themselves.[7] They did not believe, a church official told the *New York Evening Telegram* in 1903, that a parent simply has the right to "sacrifice" a child "to his own belief . . . . I would state without reservation that he has no such right." [8] But neither did they feel that conscientious reliance on spiritual instead of medical means for healing should automatically be defined by the law as neglect. Their position, which sought a balance between parental and state responsibilities, received considerable support in the press, and eventually in the law. The newspaper publisher William Randolph Hearst, a nonadherent, wrote about one "miracle" in which his own infant son, in critical condition because of a closed pylorus but considered too frail to survive an operation, was healed overnight after a Christian Science practitioner was called in as a last resort.[9] Similar experiences led other parents to feel the same kind of gratitude. Rightly or wrongly, Christian Scientists maintained that their overall record in the care of children was comparable to care rendered by others. They held that decisions on treatment of their own children should be left to the children's "natural guardians, who are at the bedside and to whom the little one's life means more than it does to all other persons."[10]

When the distinguished medically trained philosopher William James broke with his peers to testify against a medical bill targeted at Christian Science in Massachusetts, he confided to a friend that he "never did anything that required as much moral effort" in his life. "Bah! I'm sick of the whole business," he wrote in 1898, "and I well know how all my colleagues at the Medical School, who go only by the label, will view me and my efforts." James found the prevailing "medical materialism" in the orthodox practice of the profession inadequate. He was neither versed in nor drawn to the theories of the Christian Scientists, but as an exponent of pragmatism in medicine as well as philosophy he saw their "facts" as "startling" and did not wish to see closed a potential avenue of healing: "Why this mania for more laws? Why seek to stop the really extremely important experiences which these peculiar creatures are rolling up?"[11]

Few critics charged that testimonies published in the church's periodicals were dishonest, but from a medical perspective they were hardly written with laboratory exactitude. By their nature they involved life situations rather than clinical case studies. Traditional doctors produced a veritable subgenre of popular articles "debunking" these testimonies and attributing the phenomena of healing to a standard litany of causal factors: time, suggestion, *vis medicatrix naturae*, the placebo effect, misdiagnosis, the power of will. The challenge to the profession, Dr. John Chadwick Oliver told colleagues in 1899, was to have charity for the Christian Scientists' superstitions and "educate and enlighten" them as to the "real foundation" of their experiences.[12]

The question would not be resolved so easily. Christian Scientists maintained that their practice was often dismissed by the medical profession irrespective of results because it challenged conventional methods. As Clifford Smith remarked, it was often simply assumed "that the drug system is scientific in its practice and certain in its results; that Christian Science does not heal anybody, or if it did, they were not sick; that Christian Scientists are actuated by religious fanaticism and not by reason and convincing experience. . . . "[13]

The situation was complicated both by the dramatic publicity given individual failures and the frequent misattribution to Christian Science of cases in which it was involved marginally if at all—as in the death of the American novelist Harold Frederic in 1898, which became something of a medical *cause celebre.* On the other hand, it was undeniable that a large number of those who testified to healings in Christian Science had turned to it in what were to all appearances circumstances in which attending physicians had given up.

Medical practitioners themselves faced an ethical challenge in maintaining objectivity when evaluating a massive body of testimony that ran contrary to their predilections. In 1907, the *Journal of the American Medical Association* published a detailed medical history of an unexplained case believed to be the "first instance recorded of recovery from generalized blastomycosis,"[14] but refused to print a letter from the husband of the patient pointing out that the recovery took place only when a Christian Science practitioner was called.[15]

Alfred Farlow noted sensibly enough that "the recitation of Christian Science healings" even with scientific diagnosis does not answer the question of their medical significance, though it points to the breadth of the experience on which Christian Scientists' convictions—and their claim to legal toleration—have been based.[16] People might differ as to the explanation for these results, Farlow acknowledged, but that there were results not easily explained away he saw as more than a matter of purely subjective faith. As the early controversy over the movement abated, the practice of spiritual healing became less a topic of headlines, but it continued as a quiet way of life in many thousands of Christian Science families—a collective "test" of spiritual healing on an unprecedented scale.

[1] Reprinted from *New York Morning Telegraph.* "Christian Science and Legislation." Boston, 1909:128.

[2] As to Legislation. *Christian Science Sentinel,* February 5, 1903; 5:360.

[3] Smith, Clifford P. *Christian Science: Its Legal Status.* Boston, 1914:35.

[4] Eddy, Mary Baker. *The First Church of Christ, Scientist, and Miscellany.* The First Church of Christ, Scientist, Boston, 1913:220.

[5] Reprinted from *Boston Post. Christian Science Sentinel,* 1900:2:453.

[6] Cf. Massachusetts Department of Public Health. "Christian Science and Community Medicine." *New England Journal of Medicine,* 1974; 290:401–2.

[7] Farlow, Alfred. "Plea for Toleration of their Honest Beliefs." *Christian Science Sentinel,* 1900:2:469.

[8] McCrackan, William D. "Freedom of Choice." Reprinted from *New York Evening Telegram. Christian Science Sentinel,* April 11, 1903; 5:506.

[9] Hearst, William Randolph. "Faith" (pamphlet). San Simeon, California: 1941.

[10] Smith, *op cit*:54.

[11] The Letters of William James. Ed. H. James. Boston, 1920; 2:66–72.

[12] " 'Christian Science' and Allied Fads." *JAMA,* 1899; 32:1363–5.

[13] Smith, *op cit*:51.

[14] Herrick, J.B. "Generalized Blastomycosis: Report of a case with recovery." *JAMA,* 1907; 49:328.

[15] Flower, B.O. "Christian Science as a Religious Belief and a Therapeutic Agent." Boston, 1909: 105–115.

[16] Reply to Review of Rev. Lyman Powell's Book. *Boston Times.* January 11, 1908.

ANOTHER basic point needs to be taken into account when considering legislative accommodation of Christian Science healing for children: that it is one aspect of a broader pattern of recognizing spiritual healing in American society. Obviously, this recognition does not in itself "prove" the validity of Christian Science healing. But it does reflect the fact that this mode of healing has been widely regarded over the years as worthy of serious consideration by intelligent people.

A section from an *amicus curiae* ("friend of the court") brief submitted to a California court on behalf of The First Church of Christ, Scientist, by the distinguished law firm O'Melveny and Myers gives a picture of this broad and longstanding recognition of Christian Science healing.

• • •

From

Brief of *amicus curiae* on behalf of The First Church of Christ, Scientist

in support of petitioner Laurie Grouard Walker in the
Supreme Court of the State of California

T HE Christian Science approach to health care has been
widely recognized by society in general as an alternative
approach to medical care and treatment.

1. **State and Federal legislation acknowledging and accommodating Christian Science as an acceptable alternative health care response.**

At both the federal and state level, literally hundreds of
laws and regulations have been adopted which acknowledge
and accommodate the practice of Christian Science. Set
forth . . . are more than three hundred such statutes, administrative rules and regulations pertaining to spiritual healing generally, or the practice of Christian Science in particular, and
health care issues. The appended statutory compilation is by
no means exhaustive. It strongly establishes, at minimum, that
the practice of Christian Science has been accorded widespread
acknowledgement and respect by legislatures throughout the
nation. Summarized below are only a few of the more significant areas of legislative enactment.

General Practice Acts. . . . most states have laws which specifically affirm the rights of their citizens to select the means of
treatment of disease or illness in accordance with their personal dictates, religious beliefs or conscience ("right of conscience" laws). *See, e.g.,* Okla. Stat. tit. 63, §1-109 (1984). In
addition, in more specific medical treatment areas such as cancer, a number of states including California have enacted statutes which expressly exempt Christian Science practitioners
from state proscriptions against treatment by non-medical
means. *See, e.g.,* Cal. Health & Saf. Code §1709.

61

Treatment of Children. Virtually all state statutes which protect children from parental neglect and abuse make express provision for the right of parents to utilize spiritual treatment, and most expressly exclude the provision of such care as a basis for a finding of "neglect" or "abuse." *See, e.g.,* Cal. Pen. Code §§270, 1165(c)(2); Cal. Welf. & Inst. Code §§16509.1, 18950.5; N.Y. Penal Law §260.15 (McKinney 1980).

Treatment of Elderly or Incapacitated Adults. Closely paralleling the subject of child abuse legislation is the more recent development of statutory protection of elderly, incapacitated or incompetent adults. No fewer than twenty-four states, including California, have passed such statutes which include acknowledgement of the propriety of Christian Science treatment in language nearly identical to that found in child neglect and abuse statutes. *See, e.g.,* Cal. Welf. & Inst. Code §15610(c)(2); Ore. Rev. Stat §§441.680, 410.700.

Medical Assistance or Benefit Programs. Numerous state medical assistance programs cover reimbursement for treatment by spiritual means, usually with specific reference to treatment by Christian Science practitioners and nurses. *See, e.g.,* Cal. Welf. & Inst. Code §§14004, 14132. A number of states which have enacted "no-fault" automobile liability statutes similarly recognize the costs of Christian Science treatment within the definition of recoverable losses. *See, e.g.,* Fla. Stat. Ann. §627.736(1)(a) (West 1984). Additionally, the Internal Revenue Service of the federal government has for over thirty years expressly recognized expenses incurred in connection with treatment by Christian Science practitioners and nurses as legitimate deductible medical expenses on federal income tax returns. *See* Rev. Rul. 55-261, 1955-18 I.R.B. 18; IRS Publication 17 (Rev. Nov. 85) . . . .

Occupational Health and Safety. Numerous job disability and worker's compensation laws expressly permit an employee's injury or illness to be certified by Christian Science practitioners. *See, e.g.,* Md. Code Ann., Art. 64A, §37(a)(3)(ii) (Supp. 1985); Tenn. Code Ann. §§8-38-125(2), 8-50-101(b)(1).

2. Recognition of Christian Science healing in insurance.

There is also widespread recognition by the insurance industry of Christian Science healing as an acceptable alternative treatment for health problems. Nearly all of the 300 major health insurance companies in this country include coverage of Christian Science care and treatment under their individual and group health insurance policies . . . . The federal government's Indemnity Benefit Plan, administered by The Aetna Life Insurance company, which provides health insurance for all federal civil service employees, authorizes benefits for Christian Science care and treatment, including reimbursement for practitioner fees, care at a Christian Science nursing facility and services of Christian Science nurses . . . . Other forms of recognition of Christian Science healing by the federal and state government in the area of insurance include health insurance provided by the federal government for members of the United States uniformed services and dependents, and provision by California, as well as at least thirteen other states, of group health and accident insurance for state and local employees which include payments for Christian Science care and treatment.

As noted above, many states have enacted compulsory automobile insurance laws, which provide coverage for Christian Science care and treatment. In those states which do not have compulsory automobile insurance laws, the auto insurance industry universally recognizes coverage for Christian Science benefits. In 1973, the Insurance Services Offices, which is the national rating bureau for member auto casualty underwriters, reaffirmed its position that Christian Science benefits, in lieu of medical benefits, would be covered under all automobile insurance policies . . . .

The above is only a partial summary of statutory law and insurance provisions which recognize Christian Science healing as a legitimate alternative to medical treatment. They reflect the strong and consistent intent of the Congress and of state legislatures to preserve to Christian Scientists the guarantee of free exercise of religious rights accorded all persons under the United States Constitution. They also reflect a well-founded recognition that Christian Scientists have historically cared for themselves and their families in a way that society finds acceptable. Since Christian Scientists have been a relatively well-known and widely dispersed religious group since the early years of this century, the fact that they have not been conspicuous for ill health confirms the reasonableness of this recognition.

THE brief from which the previous section was taken concluded with the following statement about two cases against Christian Scientist parents before California courts:

"This case admittedly poses troubling and emotional issues for the Court. The death of any child is a tragic loss, and one which is felt by no one more than by parents who loved and cared for their child as best they could. Each day in this State, parents lose children to disease and sickness, most in hospitals or under care of medical doctors who work unsuccessfully to save them through medical science. Those parents bear quietly the grief of their great loss. In these proceedings, the tragedies of two children's deaths have been compounded by the prosecution of parents who deeply loved and cared for their child, and who believed sincerely that they were doing what was best for the health and recovery of their child. The actions of these Christian Scientist parents, taken in good faith and in accordance with deeply-held religious beliefs, is not the sort of conduct to which the manslaughter or felony child abuse statutes of this State were directed."

These words point to an acutely felt dilemma now before society. Whether Christian Science healing for children should be accommodated by law, or whether its practice should be prohibited and parents who have lost children under spiritual treatment prosecuted, has become a widely discussed issue. It raises serious ethical and religious questions. And it also involves basic constitutional issues on the relation of religion and the state in the light of First Amendment freedoms.

An article by David Williams, the Church's representative on federal questions in Washington, D.C., outlines Christian Scientists' approach to these constitutional issues. The article was written for the magazine *Church and State*, published by Americans United for the Separation of Church and State.

• • •

Christian Science and the care of children: the constitutional issues

David N. Williams

in *Church and State*, September 1989

CHILDREN'S health care has become a major issue on the national agenda in recent years.

For those who care about the First Amendment as well as families, one particular aspect of this issue has presented something of a moral dilemma: the care of children whose parents rely on healing prayer in time of sickness. Six cases now in the courts have focused attention on this issue as it relates to Christian Scientists, a group long known both for the practice of spiritual healing and for a strong tradition of family life.

Should spiritual healing as Christian Scientists practice it be accommodated in state law, or should that practice be restricted by state statute and parents who have lost children under spiritual treatment be subject to criminal prosecution? Americans should consider the following points as they seek to answer that question.

The formation of public policy should not begin with the premise that such healing is irrelevant or imaginary—which would pit the state against religious life—but should broadly and fairly reflect actual experience. Yet behind the current prosecutions of Christian Science parents is the assumption that reliance on healing through prayer is the equivalent of "martyring" children. Prosecutors in these cases have often cited the legal principle that parents can "martyr themselves for religious reasons, but have no right to martyr their children."

That is a well-founded principle as it applies to religious practices that *are* harmful or irresponsible. What has not been considered is the possibility that serious spiritual healing might not belong in that category—that the benefits for turning consistently to this way of healing might be real and significant.

As both an ethical and constitutional principle, Christian Scientists agree that the responsibility of parents to maintain the health and welfare of children is primary. The question is whether a religious mode of healing and caring for children should be ruled out essentially because it *is* religious. The constitutional issue in the current debate over spiritual healing for children revolves around the free exercise and establishment clauses of the First Amendment: "Congress shall make no law respecting an establishment of religion or prohibiting the free exercise thereof." But *no one*—Christian Scientists included— is saying that parents' religious freedom supervenes children's right to live, or that the First Amendment, or any legal or religious principle, entitles them or others to "martyr" children on the altar of their religious beliefs.

Those who maintain that the state should prohibit the practice of spiritual healing for children frequently cite the Supreme Court decision in *Reynolds v. United States* (1879) to the effect that while the right of religious belief is absolute and unrestricted, the right to act on religious belief is not. While limitations on religious practice are sometimes warranted, high court decisions since *Reynolds* have included repeated reminders that it is the clear intent of the Constitution to protect the "free *exercise* of religious belief" and not just belief itself. And as established in *Sherbert v. Verner* (1963) and subsequent cases, the state must prove a truly compelling interest in restricting any religious practice, showing that no less restrictive means "are available to achieve" that interest.

In other words, First Amendment rights are so basic to society that free exercise must be guarded up to the very point at which overriding state interest compels us to place these limits. In view of the fundamental role in our tradition of the right of free exercise, the burden of proof that the state has a compelling interest to restrict Christian Science healing for children must lie on the opponents of that practice who wish their view written into law.

Granting that the state's duty to protect the health of children is sufficiently basic to override free exercise of religious belief, does that duty in the case of Christian Scientists' children warrant restriction of the practice of spiritual healing on their behalf?

Any defensible answer to this question must be based on more than mere assumptions plucked from the air of the current views within a segment of our society. Even taking into account recent medical advances, insofar as the law is concerned, a method of treatment must be judged by its results rather than by the *a priori* assumption that one method is inherently superior to another.

Over the twenty-year period from 1969 to 1988, for example, *The Christian Science Journal* and the *Christian Science Sentinel* published over 7,100 testimonies of physical healings. While these accounts are definitely religious documents rather than clinical histories, some 2,338 of the healings described involved medically diagnosed conditions. In many more cases the testimonies implied that there had been diagnosis but did not specifically state it. Many—literally hundreds—of the diagnoses involved x-rays or were confirmed by second opinions by specialists or other physicians.

The range of conditions healed included congenital, degenerative, infectious, neurological, and other disorders, some considered terminal or incurable. These testimonies included over 2,400 healings of children. More than 600 of these involved medically diagnosed conditions, life-threatening as well as less serious, including spinal meningitis (in several cases after antibiotics failed to help), pneumonia and double pneumonia, diabetes, food poisoning, heart disorders, loss of eyesight from chemical burns, pleurisy, stomach obstruction, epilepsy, goiter, leukemia, malaria, mastoiditis, polio, rheumatic fever, and ruptured appendix.

Obviously, these healings represent a body of individual cases rather than controlled experimental results. By its sheer volume and variety, however, this body of cases underscores the fact that healing in Christian Science has been regular and tangible—not the exception—and that it cannot be dismissed as merely "doing nothing" or waiting on natural processes.

Christian Scientists acknowledge that failures have occurred under their form of treatment just as they have under medical care, in pediatric as in other kinds of cases. Physicians argue, understandably, that some who have died might have been saved under their care. Yet there is no evidence that disproportionate numbers of Christian Scientists' children have been lost. In fact, such figures as are available would indicate that the very opposite is the case.

Christian Scientists feel that a greater number of children would, in effect, have been "martyred" to medical technology if their parents hadn't had the freedom to turn in a wholly different, spiritual direction for healing. The small number of deaths of children in Christian Science families are clearly *exceptions*—no less tragic than similar occurrences under medical care, but also no more common proportionately and no more criminal.

Taking account of the positive evidence for spiritual healing and other available indications of its relative healing record in comparison to medical treatment, it cannot plausibly be maintained that there is a compelling state interest in restricting Christian Science practice for children. Laws in most states have traditionally sought a balance between accommodation of responsible spiritual healing and the power of the courts to order medical treatment in extreme individual cases. This balance preserves the state's authority under the doctrine of *parens patriae*, while recognizing that there has not been a demonstrable compelling interest which would warrant drastically restricting spiritual healing for children across the board.

Still, Christian Scientists would by no means wish a general legal accommodation to furnish an umbrella for the protection of non-medical healing that the state may well have a compelling reason to restrain. There are fundamental differences among the various groups that practice some form of non-medical healing. A growing consensus, including Christian Scientists, holds that God's will is always for life and healing and approaches the healing ministry on the basis of this conviction. But some who practice what is conventionally known as "faith healing" accept disease and death as God's will when a healing does not occur.

Many, however, ask how our laws functioning under the First Amendment can implement state accommodation of responsible spiritual healing, without at the same time protecting any and every kind of religious healing, regardless of whether it can provide the kind of creditable record that justifies such protection. There is a well-established tradition, based on such Supreme Court decisions as *Wisconsin v. Yoder,* for legal accommodation of special needs of such diverse religious groups as the Amish, the Seventh-day Adventists, Jews, and Roman Catholics. But can the state implement the free exercise clause of the First Amendment without violating the nonestablishment clause that directly precedes it?

If the issue were simply a matter of choosing between the merits of different *faiths,* the answer in constitutional terms must be clear and unequivocal: There is no constitutional basis for such discrimination, which would clearly violate the establishment clause of the First Amendment. If, however, grounds for accommodation were strictly *secular*—i.e., that all who sought it must give reasonable evidence of providing children with a responsible system of health care—the criteria for recognition would be secular and not religious, and no violation of the establishment clause would be involved.

These criteria constitute an ethic of responsibility for all who practice spiritual healing for children. On this basis, the hard-won legal right to practice spiritual healing does not provide unlimited license nor does it reflect state bias in anyone's favor. Rather, it reflects the warranted acknowledgment that parents can provide spiritual care for children in a context that fulfills the commonly acknowledged secular standard of responsibility.

Those who are uncomfortable with provisions recognizing responsible spiritual healing for children might wish to consider the alternative: If the state discriminated against such healing—not because it was ineffectual but only because it was not medical (at least in the conventional sense)—the result would be significant growth in the already discernible tendency for the state to become not only the prisoner but the *agent* of the secular assumptions of a portion of our society. As a May 1 editorial in *The Cincinnati Enquirer* noted, one of the current prosecutions of Christian Science parents "deserves watching for what it may signal about society's ability to substitute its precepts for religion's."

For this reason, all citizens, not just Christian Scientists or other advocates of spiritual healing, have a compelling interest in ensuring that our laws do not needlessly discriminate against religion and translate the secular assumptions of some into laws that all are compelled to obey.

4

How would restricting Christian Science healing for children affect society?

As Christian Scientists have often pointed out, the current debate over their practice of spiritual healing for children involves far more than the interests of a single denomination. It involves serious and far-reaching questions about the direction society is taking: about attitudes towards family, the limits of government, the role of medicine, and the future of religion. This final section touches on these long-range questions, and it includes expressions of opinion and concern by Christian Scientists and non-Christian Scientists alike.

For many, a primary problem arising from attempts to restrict spiritual healing for children is what it signifies about the intrusion of government in matters affecting choices within families and the exercise of religious belief. For example, a column in a Christian periodical reflecting a very different theological perspective from Christian Science, spoke of the need for "parents to take the lead in spiritual nurture" of children. And of the parents it specifically commented: "Those who would charge them with child abuse or criticize them for living out their religion as a family understand neither the nature of the family nor of religion" ("Crimes of Faith?," *Christianity Today*, June 16, 1989, p. 71).

The first two items in this section are editorials reflecting the Christian Science viewpoint on the question of government intrusion on issues involving family and religion. One is from a Church publication, the other is a guest column written for a major newspaper by the Church's Committee on Publication Manager.

• • •

For the sake of family, for the sake of humanity

Allison W. Phinney, Jr.

in the *Christian Science Sentinel*, May 16, 1988, pp. 25–28

N OT everyone has had the experience of growing up in a strong and loving family. Even so, many people feel pretty deeply about the subject.

It shows in their tendency to create family groupings wherever and whenever they can. Sometimes a sports team, for example, or office workers at their best take on the feeling of family.

Families can accomplish something that no bureaucracy or government agency can ever achieve. It's a lot more than a cliché to say it is in a family setting that moral and spiritual values are most effectively nurtured. No country can legislate a moral climate that produces a citizenry imbued with honesty, moral courage, self-sacrifice. But the laws of a country can provide families with the room and the right to work toward that end.

Nowadays, though, there seems to be a trend moving powerfully in the opposite direction. The state tends more and more to take the role of "father knows best"—under a doctrine of jurisprudence called *parens patriae*.

If we look at the bleak statistics of child abuse, at the harsh human situations of families gone wrong, where there is no parental sense of responsibility to build on, all this might seem simple necessity. Who wouldn't be moved to tears and to action by thousands of cases of neglect, abuse, and sheer ignorance? Yet it is also equally clear that policing by the state in such circumstances should be a last resort. It must not be an avid enthusiasm for substituting the authority of the state for the role of the parent.

Suppose, however, that under pressure for increasing public regulation of private lives by a government, conventional medical care is mandated, and then that people are closely watched to see they supply it. Suppose, for instance, that federal regulations were to be established requiring every state in the United States to override parental judgment and provide medical care "to the child when his health requires it." In the broadest terms this would mean that Christian Scientists, for whom the healing presence of God is a practical reality, are no longer to believe in divine power. Or, at least, what they believe, they are no longer to act upon. They must, in effect, turn their family over to the judgment of the state and to material medicine as the only means of proper care. And if the laws of the states do not incorporate reporting regulations which demand this, then the states will not be eligible for federal financing.

What would be the effect of such regulations on these deeply responsible and moral families, many in their fifth generation of commitment to Christian Science? Wouldn't it strike at the spiritual center of the family, aggressively, intrusively undermining the understanding of God as having any significant import in human affairs?

Is this a far-fetched futuristic scenario? No. Similar requirements that all parents provide medical care are already in place in Great Britain. And regulations at the federal level now exist in the United States. These regulations, coupled with a new aggressive campaign of legal prosecution and pressure, would threaten to overturn existing religious provisions. Such provisions have been included over the years throughout the United States and elsewhere to protect the religious rights of Christian Scientists and others to seek an effective spiritual approach to healing.

It was in a far different climate of constitutional guarantees of freedom of religious practice that Christian Science, devoted to reinstating the power and practice of original Christianity, was first able to put down roots and grow. Mary Baker Eddy, who discovered and founded Christian Science, could write confidently some eight decades ago: "The Constitution of the United States does not provide that *materia medica* shall make laws to regulate man's religion; rather does it imply that religion shall permeate our laws. Mankind will be God-governed in proportion as God's government becomes apparent, the Golden Rule utilized, and the rights of man and the liberty of conscience held sacred." [1]

The decline of seriously held religious values, and with it the erosion of individual freedoms, might have been difficult to conceive eighty years ago. But society has now come to the point where it must ask itself some very sobering questions. Is God going to be tolerated only as a kind of inspirational poetry? Are we truly ready to decide that the teachings of Christ Jesus regarding prayer and healing are no longer to be allowed to be taken seriously in a materialistic, technocratic society? As *Science and Health with Key to the Scriptures* by Mrs. Eddy points out: "Denial of the possibility of Christian healing robs Christianity of the very element, which gave it divine force and its astonishing and unequalled success in the first century." [2] Is society ready to take the long, decisive step into a night of secularism by throwing its weight wholly on the side of materialism over against any hope of practical Christianity?

Before such a step is conclusively taken, it needs to be understood thoroughly where this may well be leading in regard to individual freedoms, not simply in regard to the rights of a religious minority. It is, after all, the concept of man as having spiritual individuality that undergirds strong convictions of the rights of the individual.

The truth is that the present trend, which seems so commanding, is by no means irreversible. If those who are committed to the continuance of Christianity as practical and viable even in a scientific age are fully wakened to the significance of the hour, the mental climate can change.

The fact is that never before in history has there been such widespread questioning of the definition of man as wholly material. There is a new thirst for the fulfillment that only morality and spirituality afford. And not in fifty years has there been such stir and shifting in the medical world itself, as it tries to assimilate remarkable new discoveries of the mental sources of disease.

This is no time to be seeking some bland protective coloration, some withdrawal from the rest of society. Now is the time to understand the true dimensions of these issues.

[1] *The First Church of Christ, Scientist, and Miscellany*, p. 222.
[2] *Science and Health*, p. 134.

"Let Parents Protect Their Children's Health"

Nathan A. Talbot

in *USA TODAY*, May 4, 1988

AMERICANS are traditionally wary of too much state intrusion into family life. Children thrive in strong and loving families, and society thrives when families thrive. Few question the need in today's world for the state to support and provide room for the nurturing that families do best.

Few also question the important role of the state in protecting children, especially since social changes have put the family structure under strain. But in a society as diverse as ours, with many differing views on what's best for children, a careful line needs to be drawn between protecting children from irresponsible parents and forcing "state" opinions too zealously on responsive parents.

An editorial in the *Christian Science Sentinel* put it this way: "If we look at the bleak statistics of child abuse, at the harsh human situations of families gone wrong . . . [the trend toward state intervention] might seem simple necessity. Who wouldn't be moved to tears and to action by thousands of cases of neglect, abuse and sheer ignorance? Yet it is equally clear that policing by the state in such circumstances should be a last resort. It must not be an avid enthusiasm for substituting the authority of the state for the role of the parent."

In health care, the pendulum has swung toward avid enthusiasm for state-controlled choices. Often, the label of neglect is applied even to informed parents who care deeply about their children but who differ with prevailing views on the kind of care that can help most. In recent years, this has happened particularly with Christian Scientists' longstanding practice of spiritual healing. This practice is a religious choice, but also a free choice based on love and experience rather than merely on faith.

For Christian Scientists, spiritual healing involves taking active responsibility for their children's well-being. That explains why tragedies involving children have been so much the exception in their experience (though these tend to be all that's reported in the news). It also explains the substantial and growing evidence of actual healings—not just one-shot "miracles"—in the several hundred thousand families raised under conscientious Christian Science care over the past decades.

Someone—either parents or a state bureaucracy—has to make decisions for young children. The choices aren't always clear-cut. Medical tragedies occur daily. Given the sensitiveness of these decisions, they're best left as fully as possible in the hands of loving parents—including those parents practicing responsible spiritual healing in the context of this love.

For other commentators on this issue, restricting Christian Science practice for children or prosecuting parents who have lost children is disturbing for a different reason. It signals what they see as a further example of the erosion of religious liberty in our society through unwarranted governmental action. As discussed earlier, Christian Scientists believe that First Amendment rights to "free exercise of religious beliefs," together with their good record of care for children, legitimatizes legal accommodation of their form of healing. They acknowledge that First Amendment rights are not absolute. But they also maintain with others that these rights are of such vital importance that it should require a compelling state interest to override them. Given the overall good record of Christian Science healing in caring for children, no such interest has been demonstrated.

Many others, while sometimes disagreeing with Christian Scientists' beliefs and practices, have also been disturbed at the potential erosion of constitutional freedom signified by prosecution of Christian Scientists and government restriction of their healing practice. Several representative statements reflect this concern. The last of these is an editorial from the denomination's newspaper, *The Christian Science Monitor.*

• • •

Letter to the editor

Robert L. McCollom, M.D.

Sarasota Herald–Tribune (Sarasota, Florida), January 3, 1989

OUR heartfelt sympathy goes out to William and Christine Hermanson, charged with murder for the sudden death of their beloved 7-year-old daughter, Amy, when she became ill two years ago.

Amy evidently came down with a sore throat and, after a short illness, lapsed into a coma and died. An autopsy disclosed that she died of juvenile diabetes.

It should be noted that Amy's parents did not know or realize that Amy was suffering from juvenile diabetes, a very serious illness with a high mortality rate, even in the care of experienced physicians. Many times in children, or adults, diabetes is not diagnosed until it is too late to cure. If the diagnosis is made in early childhood, lives may be saved by continuous treatment.

Amy's Christian Scientist parents, in accordance with their religious beliefs, chose prayer instead of medical treatment. For this they are charged with third-degree murder and felony child abuse.

These charges never should have been brought in the first place. If the prosecutors and judiciary in this case are consistent in their murder and child-abuse charges, they should start prosecuting for child abuse and murder the parents of children who have died of alcohol and drug abuse, auto accidents, suicide, etc. Parents of many children on drugs have failed to take their children to doctors, drug rehabilitation centers, or to have their children tested for drugs in order to save their lives.

Obviously, prosecuting such parents is ridiculous. They have lost loved ones and they are not murderers. Neither are the Hermansons.

These charges defy the basic American right to practice freedom of religion as guaranteed by our Constitution. Who is to tell people what religious beliefs they must follow?

For over 1900 years, people of the Christian faith relied mainly on prayers to God to see them through problems and illnesses; they still rely on them today. The medical profession has come a long way in the last century, but it is not God, and not the answer to all illnesses.

The legal profession and courts cannot eliminate the value of prayer, central to many faiths around the world, in isolated court cases.

It has been my privilege to briefly meet William and Christine Hermanson, their lovely son and newborn son. They are fine, devoted parents and sincere in their religious beliefs. I would rate them with any parents in Sarasota.

They are definitely not murderers or child abusers, and neither are Christian Scientists. They are kind, God-loving people and parents.

If the 12th Circuit prosecutors are looking for prestige or business, they should devote some attention to preventing parents with AIDS from passing on the virus to their babies, the equivalent of a death sentence. Further measures are needed to keep parents suffering from drug addictions from passing those to newborns, which also may mean ruined lives, or a death sentence. Further testing for an early diagnosis of diabetes and drug abuse on children of all ages is recommended. It will save many lives.

For the Hermansons, who have suffered enough from these unwise proceedings, I suggest as a (belated) Christmas present that all charges be dropped.

Letter to the editor

Janet B. O'Neil

The Florida Times-Union (Jacksonville, Florida), June 17, 1989

I HOPE I'm not the only person who is upset about the verdict rendered by the state of Florida against William and Christine Hermanson, the Christian Scientist couple who chose Christian Science healing instead of conventional medical treatment for their sick child who subsequently died.

While I am not a Christian Scientist, I am a religious-minded person, with a lot of faith in God, and I, too, try to practice what I preach in my daily life. I hope that I would have the courage, should the circumstances arise, to give my very life for the right to my religious beliefs.

I believe the Hermansons were acting in good faith when they made a decision on the medical treatment they wanted for their child.

And I also believe "The State" has drastically over-stepped the bounds separating church and state, as defined in the U.S. Constitution by sitting in judgment of those people for that decision.

This is a religious issue, and the decision made by the State violates the Hermansons' right to freedom of religious beliefs and practices.

What bothers me the most is thinking, where will this end? Today, it has been decided that Christian Scientists can no longer follow the dictates of their faith when it comes to medical treatment for their children, which is an area absolutely central to their religious doctrine.

What if tomorrow, the State decides that I, as a Catholic, can no longer "deprive" my children of red meat during Lent? Or that my neighbor, who is Jewish, can no longer circumcise his male children? Or that my cousin, who is Baptist, can no longer immerse his children in water to baptize them?

I think this is one area in which we of different persuasions ought to lay aside our differences and unite as voters to make our voices heard. Because if we don't where will it end?

Healing: a Christian Science conviction raises serious legal questions

Editorial

The Cincinnati Enquirer, May 1, 1989

THE conviction of Mr. and Mrs. William Hermanson of contributing to the death of their daughter has significance far beyond the Sarasota, Fla., courtroom in which their trial unfolded. There are at least half a dozen similar cases going to trial soon, and the pattern established in the Hermanson case, if not overturned, could influence decisions in the others.

The Hermansons' 7-year-old daughter died in September, 1986, of complications from diabetes. As practicing Christian Scientists, Mr. and Mrs. Hermanson did not seek conventional medical care for her; they relied instead on the services of a Christian Science practitioner. The prosecutor in Sarasota argued that their decision amounted to child abuse and third-degree murder, and the jury agreed.

The Hermansons were prosecuted under a curious Florida statute that holds anyone who "through willful or culpable negligence" withholds medical treatment from a child is guilty of criminal child abuse. The Hermansons, in their defense, cited another Florida law, which declared that parents who, for religious reasons, do not provide medical care for a child may not, for that reason alone, be considered "abusive or neglectful."

Christian Scientists believe in the efficacy of prayer as a healing force, and the history of the church is full of instances in which seemingly miraculous cures occurred without medical intervention. Still, they are not barred from seeking conventional medical help if they choose. To say that seeking spiritual healing amounts to criminal neglect, or worse, would seem to be asserting that Christian Scientists may not practice their faith, despite the First Amendment's clear mandate.

As a practical matter, the Hermansons might have sought

conventional medical treatment that failed to save their daughter. Who would have been guilty then? The parents? The medical practitioner? Or no one? Would it simply have been a case in which medicine failed?

What, if anything, happens next in the Hermanson case deserves watching for what it may signal about society's ability to substitute its precepts for religion's.

Religion: real or show?

Editorial

Mooresville Tribune (Mooresville, North Carolina), August 23, 1989

THE Tennessee embryos-custody trial, the abortion argument rekindled by the U.S. Supreme Court and an epidemic of child-abuse stories worked this summer to draw attention from an equally heartrending three-week trial in California.

A Christian Science couple was convicted of child endangerment, a felony. Mark and Susan Rippberger were indicted more than four years ago after their nine-month-old daughter died. They were acquitted of involuntary manslaughter and found guilty of the lesser crime.

Their crime? They relied on the teachings of their church for help in time of trouble. When their child became ill they depended on spiritual healing rather than medical science. Their choice of treatment failed.

This, too, is some tough call. Right up there with the physical and theological status of embryos and fetuses.

The result of their trial clarifies nothing and signifies everything. On one level it says that people are subject to majority rule at all levels. Conventional wisdom holds that medical science is an essential part of health care. Yet nearly all professing Christians who hold this view publicly endorse the healing power of prayer.

No one in the California courtroom could doubt the depth of love the Rippbergers felt for their child. Everyone agreed the parents were convinced they were doing what was best for their daughter.

Their conviction, then, becomes a condemnation of their choice of treatment. If they had taken the child to a medical doctor and she had died, nothing would have happened to them beyond the grief of their loss.

By pinning a criminal label on the Rippbergers, the state, in effect, questions the sincerity of all professing Christians. The "prayer lists" of ailing members maintained by mainline churches become public shows of concern and nothing more. The purpose of hospital chaplains easily can be studied in this school of thought.

Of course "conventional" Christians insist man's medicine and God's grace make a team that is the best we can field against physical failing. But the California court says we really don't believe the spiritual part, we merely go through the motions for what we see as the emotional benefit of others.

In a recent editorial look at the Rippberger trial, The Christian Science Monitor poses the big question raised by its result:

"Is religion simply a kind of obsolete cultural window dressing, to be tolerated only insofar as it isn't taken too seriously? Are religious differences permissible only on matters that make no practical difference?"

Serious questions, those. Not serious theological questions. Serious questions about the role of the state in refining its responsibility and defining religion's place in it. A question of First Amendment dimensions, if you will.

Speaking for children

Editorial

The Christian Science Monitor, August 17, 1989

In the wake of a grueling three-week trial of a Christian Science couple in California, the American tradition of religious tolerance seems considerably more tenuous.

The case was the second of its kind to be tried in recent months and one of a handful currently in the courts. The couple, Mark Rippberger and Susan Middleton-Rippberger, were indicted over four years ago for turning to the practice of spiritual healing in Christian Science rather than to medical care when their nine-month-old daughter, Natalie, became ill. The tragedy of her death was caught up in a highly public debate on the relationship between the state, the family, and religious life.

The parents' acquittal on the charge of involuntary manslaughter reflected recognition at least of their deep love for their children.

Hearing Mark Rippberger's moving testimony on the witness stand, no one could doubt their love or their tender and ceaseless attentiveness to Natalie during her illness. Their conviction on the lesser charge of felony child endangerment, however, raises disturbing questions about the readiness of many to restrict the *expression* of that love when it differs with conventional majority opinion, especially in regard to conventional medicine.

Legally, the endangerment verdict was a judgment on the couple's choice of healing method rather than its results. Prosecutions under this law would make serious reliance on spiritual healing for one's children a criminal offense without considering whether such healing is actually effective and can be intelligently practiced.

There were other disturbing aspects of the trial. The prosecutor's unhidden antagonism toward Christian Science turned the case into what one nonreligious observer called a virtual "heresy trial." Deputy District Attorney David Dunn inveighed against healing prayer as a "19th-century treatment." But he showed little understanding either of what the conscientious discipline of such prayer in Christian Science involves or of what it has meant—the broad experience of healing—in many thousands of families.

This points to the deeper issue involved in these court cases. As the 21st century approaches, is religion simply a kind of obsolete cultural window dressing, to be tolerated only insofar as it isn't taken too seriously? Are religious differences permissible only on matters that make no practical difference? The movement to repress religious healing, as a Christian Scientist has written elsewhere, seeks to mete out punishment "to those who have practical expectations from religion."

During his closing arguments to the jury, the prosecutor placed a large poster with the question "Who Speaks for Natalie?" prominently on display. The question deserves profound reflection rather than manipulative courtroom theatrics. The right to "speak" for children is not earned by dogmatic assertion, secular or religious, but only by compassionate commitment to the hard work of healing and caring from day to day. That commitment is not monopolized by those whose orientation is to medical care, any more than healing itself is.

In a society struggling with the consequences of widespread parental irresponsibility—where one encounters almost daily reports of addicted or damaged or unwanted newborns—there's far more to be said for spiritual healing and the life-affirming values that underlie it than the verdict in this case implies. The continuing challenge for those whose practice is affected by it will be to earn public tolerance by virtue of their wisdom, love, and healing works.

YET another serious implication of current prosecutions and potential restrictions on Christian Scientists' healing practice is the potential for medical domination of our society. Christian Scientists have often stressed what they have in common with the medical profession: the compassionate desire to relieve human suffering. Most thoughtful expressions of concern about medical domination of social policy have come from medical professionals themselves, as well as others who believe in the benefits of medicine, but also feel that it cannot claim to be the final arbiter of Americans' health care choices. This is by no means a majority viewpoint. But as the following letters and columns show, it is a current of opinion that should not be ignored.

• • •

Column

Robert Mendelsohn, M.D.

DeLand Sun News (DeLand, Florida), March 10, 1988

D EAR READER:
Attention! All you religious folks out there. The American Academy of Pediatrics is after you.

In an article in the [American Medical Association] News, Jan. 15, 1988, headlined, "AAP Assails Religious Exemptions from Care," the AAP's Committee on Bioethics recommends the elimination of statutes which allow parents to reject medical care for their children because of religious or philosophical beliefs.

The pediatricians are greatly concerned about cases of illness or death in which patients have withheld medical treatment because of their religious beliefs, even though they confess that the number of such cases is "difficult to ascertain." (Please note that the good doctors of the AAP fail to mention the number of cases of children who die because parents accept a particular medical treatment for them.)

I bring this to your attention because the pediatricians are engaging in an example of so-far-unrecognized religious warfare. Despite the tendency of doctors to call modern medicine an "inexact science" (an oxymoron, if I ever heard one), it is more accurate to say there is practically no science in modern medicine at all.

Almost everything doctors do is based on a conjecture, a guess, a clinical impression, a whim, a hope, a wish, an opinion, or a belief. Thus, medicine is not a science at all, but a belief system. Beliefs are held by every religion, including the Religion of Modern Medicine.

By attacking religious exemptions from medical care, the Religion of Modern Medicine is attempting to establish hegemony over other religions. So you and your church leaders should be concerned about this drive for power.

M.D.'s have tried this kind of strong-arm tactics against chiropractors. As a matter of fact, they have tried their best to knock that healing system right out of the box. But Federal Judge Susan Getzendanner recently put a halt to that power grab. For decades, M.D.'s have been after Jehovah's Witnesses and have held Christian Scientists in less than high esteem. And recently, as reported in this column, M.D.'s and their (Hastings Center) medical-ethicist camp-followers have decided to go after observant Jews for rejecting the concept of "brain death."

With this latest action of the AAP, will your church be next?

From

Column

Eugene D. Robin, M.D.
Stanford University Medical School
in *The Press Enterprise* (Riverside, California), June 13, 1988

A CALIFORNIA couple stands accused of criminal behavior in the death of their young daughter. The child died of meningitis and the parents, who are Christian Scientists, are accused of causing her death by not seeking medical care. There are also two other cases of Christian Scientist parents in California whose children died of meningitis and who are also being charged with criminal behavior.

I have reviewed the records of the first case and also had an opportunity to meet at length with the mother of the child. I am no legal expert but the medical facts surrounding the first case have convinced me that to hold [the child's] parents responsible for the death of the child would be a gross miscarriage of justice.

... the present trend of prosecuting Christian Scientists in medically dubious cases poses a threat to medicine. Suppose every physician who committed an error in judgment were brought to trial. Our already over-burdened court system would be taxed to the limit.

And suppose every physician whose errors led to the death of a patient was sent to jail. There would be no room to imprison all of us doctors. If we jailed all of the pediatricians who, in the past, withheld food and water from premature babies and caused death and mental retardation in thousands of infants, we might destroy the prison system.

If we brought to trial for child abuse all of the neonatal anesthesiologists who withheld anesthesia from neonates even during major surgery because they just knew the infants did not feel pain (they do), there would not be enough court judges and juries to conduct the trial. So I do wish we doctors would be more compassionate and humble and less arrogant.

I have no useful opinion on the constitutional or legal issues involved. But as someone who is not a Christian Scientist, I can see no useful purpose to society or to anyone else in prosecuting parents for what was, at worst, an error in judgment.

One might think that they have suffered enough. I wish we doctors would adopt the biblical statement: Let he that has not sinned among you cast the first stone. Prosecuting attorneys might also benefit.

Letter to the editor

Melvin A. Drake, M.D.

The Mesa Tribune (Mesa, Arizona), December 14, 1988

WE note the continued criminal prosecution of the parents of the 12-year-old girl who died from cancer of the bone. One wonders why. This prosecution is at taxpayer expense, it might seem a needless waste of money—or for what good cause is it being spent? Apparently it is an effort to make medical and surgical care, under the direction of a licensed medical doctor, mandatory as the only valid treatment for children—perhaps for any one under 21 years of age.

This is a big order. It presupposes regimentation of opinion—no differing opinions or actions allowed—under penalty of criminal prosecution. An adult can refuse such treatment for himself, but if he fails to allow or force his children to submit to the same—he thereby becomes a felon—a criminal—and is subject to prosecution and punishment, at public expense, for failure to perform his parental "duty."

What a travesty of justice this would be! In this case, the girl was 12 years old—it cannot be questioned that she would have had to be forced to submit to the amputation of her leg at the hip—with the possibility of saving her life. Many others would react the same.

Perhaps this prosecution is meant as an attack on Christian Scientists. They are entitled to their own beliefs. As a group we see them as law abiding citizens, with a relatively low morbidity and mortality rate, and a remarkably low cost of their efforts at health maintenance. In the face of the spiraling cost of medical care, perhaps that is a blessing to them. Perhaps a study should be made—perhaps medical care itself has become too complex!

Our children are a part of us. We are responsible for their care. It is the obvious duty of every parent to provide his children with the best care possible—commensurate with the parents' knowledge and belief. This, these parents did. We would have little respect for them—in fact, it would be unthinkable that they should do otherwise. Man cannot lightly violate his conscience. The parents may be guilty of error in judgment—but never of child abuse.

Letter to the editor

The Santa Rosa Press Democrat
(Santa Rosa, California), August 16, 1989

THE Rippberger family has suffered the loss of a beloved child. I can only imagine their grief and my heart goes out to them.

I cannot conceive how anyone could possibly believe that there is a case for our judicial system in this family's tragedy. I am embarrassed that my fellow citizens have behaved in such an outrageous manner. I am not ignoring the fact that a child died, but the child's death was not because the parents weren't doing everything they thought right to do.

Consider this:

I choose medical care for my sick child and he doesn't respond to treatment. I have faith that the doctor's treatment will cure. But my child dies. Am I guilty of negligence? If not, why not?

The Rippbergers practice what they believe. They have devout faith in the healing powers of God (as do most of us when all else fails) and they are being condemned for administering to their family by the tenets of their belief and faith. Their child died; this is not a crime but a tragedy. The only crime committed here is that this community is adding to this family's immeasurable grief by filing criminal charges against them.

Please consider that a cure for an illness through medicine is no more guaranteed than a cure through religion.

I am not a Christian Scientist, but I know that in practicing their religious beliefs, a practice which is guaranteed by the U.S. Constitution, this family isn't any different from a Catholic family or a Mormon family or whichever denomination one would care to name.

Not going to a doctor is not illegal.

U P to this point, these documents have pertained to issues about Christian Scientists' practice of healing for children in their bearing on American society today. Yet these issues have an even broader significance. They relate not just to social but to religious questions—to some of the deepest issues facing Christians everywhere.

The last items in this section are statements by Christian Scientists relating to these larger issues. First, a section from an article entitled "Spiritual Healing on Trial: A Christian Scientist Reports" raises serious questions about the implications of Christians' rejecting evidence for spiritual healing. The article appeared in the widely read mainstream Protestant publication *The Christian Century*. The next statement by a church spokesperson writing for a European ecumenical magazine sharpens the issue even further. The final item, an editorial from a Church publication, expresses how Christian Scientists view the larger meaning of the spiritual healing they practice in the broad context of the very future of religion.

• • •

From

"Spiritual Healing On Trial: A Christian Scientist Reports"

Stephen Gottschalk

The Christian Century, June 22–29, 1988

As Gordon Dalbey noted six years ago, "The ministry of physical healing stands in the center of our Christian faith. And yet, though the Gospels are filled with stories of healing, and the Church itself is born through an act of healing (Acts 3), most church people seem anxious to disown these stories, as if they embarrassed us" ("Recovering Christian Healing," *The Christian Century*, June 9–16, 1982).

Probably fewer church people would be embarrassed by these stories today. During this decade, the recovery of Christian healing has accelerated to the point that it has become an undeniable part of the Christian landscape. As with most grass-roots movements, it has included differing and in some instances contradictory approaches. And both Christian Science and the form of Christian healing that has become part of mainstream church life should be clearly differentiated from the "faith healing" associated with TV evangelism, itinerant evangelists (portrayed, for example, in the recent CBS television film "Promised a Miracle") and fundamentalist groups such as Faith Assembly. A recent article in a Christian Science periodical observed, "Many Christians who have ministries of healing reject the label 'faith healing.' It's becoming apparent that blind faith doesn't stand up to the scrutiny of an increasingly sophisticated and technological society" (David Brooks Andrews, "The Future of Christian Healing: Fresh Convictions and Spiritual Realism," *The Christian Science Journal*, June 1988, p. 33).

Is there a plausible basis for Christian healing? Or will Christians, by the very lack of an alternative, increasingly gravitate to the concept of a "suffering God," who suffers with us

101

in pain he is unable to prevent? Those who embrace a theology of Christian healing are not ready to sacrifice belief in God's power in order to maintain the credibility of God's love. Underlying much of Christian healing is the conviction that healing is the practical expression of God's love—of his kingdom at hand. Disease and pain are not self-evident "givens" to which we must reconcile ourselves—and our concept of God as well. Whatever the theological distance between Christian Scientists and mainstream Christians in the ministry of spiritual healing, these convictions have been at the heart of Christian Science all along.

A Methodist minister actively involved in spiritual healing for many years speaks for one current of opinion when he says, "Christian Science has been a tremendous influence because it has put its finger right on what Christ says about healing the sick. Christian Scientists have demonstrated it; they have practiced it and put it at the very heart of what they're trying to do" ("Christian Science and Spiritual Healing Today: A Conversation with the Reverend Paul Higgins," *Christian Science Sentinel*, October 6, 1986, p. 1860).

It is the successes of a healing system, not just its failures, that its opponents must reckon with. Future decades may see that reluctance to take the evidence for spiritual healing seriously as one last form of resistance to the drastic deconstruction of the mechanistic concept of reality. "Twentieth century physics," writes Robert Peel, "suggests reality may be different from that posited by the reductionist, determinist, or 'scientific' materialism of the past—and posited still by the biomedical hard-liner of today." [1] Not that the evidence for spiritual healing is itself enough to validate a theological viewpoint. Yet the cumulative weight of testimony as to its validity is more than sufficient to disrupt the complacency of a biomedical world view that would exclude it.

In view of the indictment of the Twitchells and others, assessing this evidence is far more than an intellectual exercise. The reality of spiritual healing as Christian Scientists practice it matters profoundly to those who believe it to be dangerous. It matters to Christian Scientists who see their form of healing not only as a valid and responsible form of health care but as vital to the future of Christianity.

<hr/>

[1] Robert Peel, *Spiritual Healing in a Scientific Age* (San Francisco: Harper & Row, 1987), p. 194.

Letter

Stig K. Christiansen

in *Update: A Quarterly Journal on New Religious Movements*
(September 1985), Vol. 9, No. 3, pp. 61–62

THE death of even a single child is as agonizing for Christian Scientists as it is for any others who cherish children and hold every human life sacred.

If such incidents were typical of Christian Scientists' past experience, few would remain Christian Scientists. We do not turn to spiritual healing in order to be loyal to a religious doctrine. The human situation cannot be reduced to the scenario of benighted believers versus enlightened proponents of medicine.

In fact, both sides in this exchange do agree on one crucial point. They both see compassion as the essential issue. But is this compassion merely a valuable extra in an otherwise mechanistic or biophysical process of restoring sick bodies to health? Or is the selfless love to which the New Testament bears witness actually rooted in divine love, and therefore the most powerful source of healing in human experience?

This latter contention may not seem very remarkable until one begins to take it seriously.

On what they believe to be this thoroughly biblical basis, Christian Scientists hold that the pain and suffering of the mortal condition are consequences of human blindness to the power and reality of love as revealed in the life and works of Jesus Christ. To believe less, they feel, would be virtually to lay all human tragedy at the feet of God. But fulfilling Jesus' commission to all his followers to heal the sick affirms the power of the gospel in the most practical terms.

The prayer that brings about such healing is spoken of by Christian Scientists as treatment, because they see it as a spiritual discipline which effectively eradicates the mental elements of fear, ignorance, and sin to which all human beings are subject and which lie at the root of disease.

Obviously, Christian Scientists recognize the distance they have to go in realizing the full potential of spiritual healing. But would even the most conscientious doctor claim a perfect record for the medical profession? The key point is that, for the Christian Scientist, treatment through prayer is an active process which long-term experience has shown secures remarkably consistent results. In the words of the Founder of Christian Science, it is the utilization of the power wherewith God loves us.

To deny that this power can be utilized is tantamount to denying that it exists. The debate over Christian Science healing for children, therefore, involves far more than the specifics of Christian Science theology or the evaluation of its very substantial healing record and impact on Christian healing in general. It involves the whole question of what the gospel itself means to the world if the spiritual healing it teaches is a sham and if the love supremely exemplified by Jesus cannot make a healing difference in present experience.

As thoughtful Christians have always known, living consistently in the light of this love is not easy. Christian Scientists certainly recognize how much further they have to go in this respect. In one sense it would be much easier not to make the effort. But the many who have seen or experienced the effects of such love in actual healing understandably feel it to be, in the Psalmist's words, "a present help" more basic and dependable than any other in caring for people's needs.

Christian Scientists see this insight as one which, far from being outmoded, is only just beginning to be explored.

Does religion have a future?

Allison W. Phinney, Jr.

in the *Christian Science Sentinel*, August 16, 1989, pp. 30–33

How important is religion anyway?
Religion doesn't construct buildings. Architects, engineers, steelworkers, do that.

Religion doesn't develop inventions such as computers and television.

Religion, in most of the world, doesn't govern or make laws. Parliaments, assemblies, senates, and presidents do that.

Many people would say that their religion doesn't have much bearing on their physical health, their mental health, or their marital harmony, but that in fact doctors, psychologists, and marital counselors are major factors.

Well, what do you have left? Occasional private and public prayers. A touch of church attendance. Funerals and consolation. Weddings and religious ceremonies. On that basis, is religion really a vital force in our society? Does religion have a future?

At this point probably many would begin to balk at the line of questioning. What's going on here? Why ask such questions?

The answer is that if religion is going to survive in more than museum terms, we need to be thinking a lot more seriously now about religion and what it means to us.

The seen and the unseen pressures of materialism at this time are sizable. They tell us relentlessly that man is largely a material mechanism working on the basis of soulless laws. Not just the body but human behavior in general is increasingly explained as animal and evolutionary in character. Amoral force, money, and power often appear to rule in government and business. Courts have recently moved toward making it a criminal offense if a child has passed on and the

106

parents have relied on spiritual means for the child's healing—in short, punishment is meted out to those who have practical expectations from religion.

Well, what does religion mean in contemporary life? What *can* it mean? As an example I think of a close friend. He was abandoned by his unwed mother when three or four. There were various forms of child abuse, including sexual. There was lack of food, lack of warmth, lack of human companionship. As he grew up he was physically weak, and later he was considered to have such severe learning disabilities he was barely capable of sweeping a floor. Through his prayer and his study of Christian Science he found that man actually has his intelligence and his health from God, Spirit. Today he has normal strength. He has just completed a five-year work-related course in two and a half years, with outstanding grades. You could say that his spiritual and moral progress—his religion—gave him a future.

Nor is this an isolated instance. Similar changes and healings have come into thousands of other lives through an understanding of God's goodness and power and law. Wherever there is the spirituality and godliness that make the great reality of divine good, which is God, more apparent to human thought, there is change for the better and some element of healing.

Mary Baker Eddy, who founded Christian Science, has written: "In the record of nineteen centuries, there are sects many but not enough Christianity . . . .

"A higher and more practical Christianity, demonstrating justice and meeting the needs of mortals in sickness and in health, stands at the door of this age, knocking for admission." [1] She felt Christian Science, with its healing theology, was in fulfillment of this practical Christianity. But Christianity that heals, she believed, was available to everyone and would inevitably become more widespread as the realization of the practical importance of religion began to dawn on society.

When the typical impositions on thought that have often stunted religion and made it seem a matter of ritual and ancient tradition are lifted, then the improvement it can bring to human life begins to be apparent. One effect can be awakening to the sheer practical value and necessity of morality. Another can be physical healing. And along with both can come strong new assurance of the meaningfulness of the qualities of goodness, honesty, and love, which we have intuitively trusted. People begin to see something of how misleading it is to suppose that man is merely material in origin. They catch sight of man's true nature as God's image and expression—what can be called the Science of man—and therefore see something of mankind's spiritual destiny.

"What is man, that thou art mindful of him?" asks the Psalmist in the Bible. "For thou . . . hast crowned him with glory and honour. Thou madest him to have dominion over the works of thy hands." [2]

Religion does not literally put up buildings. But in its truest form it builds up people. It shows them who and what they actually are as nothing else can.

Society benefits from practical Christianity. And Christ's Christianity has a future because it is not in fact something from the past. Wherever genuine spirituality and love for God and man have appeared in past centuries, they have been the intimation of what is to come as mankind more and more fully discerns the practicality of learning about the spiritual nature of being.

What can genuine religion do? It can keep the light in people's lives. Without acknowledgment of spiritual reality, life would become horizonless, finite, dark, and suffocating. But with a fresh recognition of God and His spiritual man we begin to have again the zeal and practicality of original Christianity. We also have light on the path into what is increasingly recognized as a spiritual era.

---

[1] *Science and Health with Key to the Scriptures*, p. 224.
[2] Ps. 8:4–6.

Appendix

Appendix

An Empirical Analysis of Medical Evidence in
Christian Science Testimonies of Healing, 1969–1988
Committee on Publication
The First Church of Christ, Scientist, Boston, Massachusetts, April 1989

[Abstract: Objective examination of religious healing is rare. A study of Christian Science testimonies of healing must be approached with caution because of the religious nature of these documents, but a large number involve medically significant conditions which are credibly diagnosed. Cumulatively assessed, these present a substantial body of experience that does not fit into a conventional medical framework. The reality of this experience as well as limits of the evidence need to be considered.]

IN July 1988 the *Southern Medical Journal* published an unusual article entitled "Positive Therapeutic Effects of Intercessory Prayer in a Coronary Care Unit." The article reported on a rigorous controlled study investigating the effects of prayer on the recovery of several hundred heart patients at San Francisco General Hospital. Christians from several denominations were asked to pray regularly for specific patients. The physician conducting the study found that the patients supported by such prayer had somewhat fewer medical complications than other patients. As one newspaper headline provocatively (if simplistically) announced, "Researcher says prayer is good for your health." [1]

The study was unusual less for its results than because it took the practice of healing prayer seriously at all. In a commentary accompanying the study, Dr. William P. Wilson of Duke University Medical Center acknowledged that the article is "likely to arouse strong prejudice in some readers who believe that religion is not worthy of scientific consideration." Nevertheless, he went on, the "questions raised seem quite valid ones for scientific inquiry. . . . It seems to me that we in medicine who claim a holistic approach to diagnosing and treating the whole man should throw away our deterministic prejudices, expand our knowledge, and enlarge our therapeutic armamentarium. We need not only a change in the way we think, but also more research on the role of religion in healing." [2]

There has been relatively little medical research on religious healing over the years, in spite of a growing body of evidence from its practice. The most substantial evidence is undoubtedly to be found in the experiences of Christian Scientists, a denomination known for its long-respected newspaper, *The Christian Science Monitor*, and committed to Christian healing practice for more than a century. Perhaps because of the strong prejudices surrounding it, this evidence is often cited by proponents or dismissed by skeptics, but rarely has it been examined objectively and analytically or considered seriously on its own terms. [3] The purpose of this study is to begin to examine the existing evidence on Christian Scientists' experience— to assess what is there as well as the questions that remain to be answered.

Background. For Christian Scientists, the practice of healing is one aspect of an active devotional life rooted in "quiet, disciplined spirituality" (as a *New York Times* religion writer recently explained) and involving considerable religious study. Their practice is unique—and still controversial—because it is not approached as merely an adjunct to medical care but as a consistent mode of treatment in its own right.

Healing is considered the effect of spiritual law, not mere personal faith. Prayer, more than an appeal for special miracles, is ongoing communion with God and openness to God's present, active love. Christian Science practitioners—individuals devoting themselves to this healing ministry as a vocation—give full time to specific prayer for church members as well as non-members who request their help.

Christian Scientists' attitude toward medical care is not based on hostility to physicians or to modern science. On the contrary, the tradition emphasizes a healthy respect for reason and education and shares compassionate values, if not methods, with all the health care professions.

Christian Scientists do not denigrate medical care for those who choose it, but they see its intense focus on the body, on physical and biochemical causes, as often reinforcing disease. It is also a focus radically different from, and not readily combinable with, a mode of healing which looks to God and spirituality as primary. For this reason, church members typically forgo medical treatment as a matter of choice and conviction, though their decisions in this regard are always their own. Christian Scientists feel spiritual healing is most effective when practiced with wholehearted devotion and, in general, significantly less effective when practiced in a context of primary reliance on medical care.

Sources.   Since 1900, some 53,900 testimonies of healing have been published in the denomination's monthly and weekly periodicals, *The Christian Science Journal* and *Christian Science Sentinel*. These testimonies are manifestly religious rather than medical documents, but the great majority relate to physical healings, and many refer to conditions that have been authoritatively diagnosed.

Their religious purpose within the denomination is to express gratitude to God and, often, to share something of the spiritual experience or regeneration behind a healing. Most, though not all, of the testifiers are Christian Scientists and members of the church. All the testimonies are submitted on the initiative of the respective testifiers, and many who have had significant physical healings in Christian Science have not submitted testimonies. One 1986 testifier healed of blindness wrote, for instance, that the experience seemed too holy to share even verbally for some time.[4] Robert Peel estimates in his 1987 work *Spiritual Healing in a Scientific Age* that only a small percentage of the actual healings in Christian Scientists' experience is recorded in written form.[5]

In form and content these accounts are as varied as the individual testifiers. Some describe particular healings in detail, while others relate more briefly a number of healings that have occurred over the course of a lifetime. It is not uncommon for a single testimony to list in passing as many as six or eight such healings, major or minor, in addition to the primary experience or experiences on which the testifier focuses. Healings merely listed without elaboration in a testimony are not included in the cumulative data given below, but they illustrate what Christian Scientists see as the normalcy of healing in the course of most adherents' lives. As one fourth-generation church member described: "Christian Science healing in our family was certainly quiet—nothing showy about it, nothing dramatic, just warm and reassuring and fairly frequent." [6]

The medical specificity of the testimonies also varies greatly. Since Christian Scientists do not routinely seek the care of physicians in time of illness, a large number of testifiers refer to healings of diseases or conditions that are not medically named. In most of these cases the conditions healed are described briefly in lay terms. In a significant proportion of other cases, however, testifiers do report specific medical diagnoses and prognoses, often explaining the circumstances in which these have been made, e.g., medical examinations required by employers, public health authorities, school officials, the military, or insurance companies; emergencies in which Christian Scientists were transported to a hospital but subsequently declined medical treatment; and situations in which individuals have turned to Christian Science for help only after unsuccessful medical treatment or prognoses of incurability.

It is fair to say in general that the emphasis of the testimonies on the spiritual dimensions of healing militates against extensive discussion of either physical symptoms or clinical histories. This is understandably frustrating to medical commentators, who have often echoed Dr. Edward Mortimer's complaint that the testimonies are merely "anecdotes." [7] Any serious study of these accounts, however, must consider them in light of what they are rather than what they are not and do not pretend to be. While their anecdotal nature is obvious, it does not in itself nullify the possible medical significance of the experiences related in them, nor does it necessarily invalidate any strictly factual evidence they contain or point to. In some cases the published testimonies give only a slight indication of the extensive medical corroboration that exists on particular healings.

One 1978 testimony in the *Christian Science Sentinel,* for ex-

ample, relates a healing of coronary artery disease for which
the testifier had been hospitalized prior to her healing in Christian Science. The one-and-a-half page *Sentinel* account is
vague in its description of the medical details, stating that a
scheduled coronary artery operation had been cancelled
abruptly because of a blood condition doctors said "made the
operation inadvisable." The testifier was told she "would be
an invalid as long as [she] lived because of the serious condition of [her] heart," but her testimony does not indicate the
specific nature of either the heart or blood condition. She goes
on to report that she turned to Christian Science several
months later and was healed within a week, and that subsequent physical examination confirmed the healing to "the
amazement of the doctor." [8]

The large medical gaps in this anecdotal account illustrate
precisely what medical readers have criticized in the Christian
Science testimonies, yet the key question for the researcher is
not how such a healing is described but what actually
occurred—the case history behind the anecdote. In this instance, when contacted for further details on her experience
several years after the testimony was published, the testifier
provided a lengthy affidavit detailing her examination and
treatment by at least six different physicians in three hospitals
and two clinics over a period of three years.[9] Whether or not
"amazement" accurately describes the last doctor's state of
mind on finding her unexpectedly healed, he was sufficiently
surprised that he sent for her records from Temple University
Hospital in Philadelphia and after reviewing them called her in
for another extensive examination. Over a decade later the
testifier obtained these records herself, at the request of the
Christian Science church. The hospital diagnosis was coronary
artery disease with obstruction of the right coronary artery,
Meniere's disease, hyperthyroidism, and an undetermined
blood disorder possibly "due to one of the medications that the
patient was on." [10]

Integrity and reliability.   Few even of the severest critics of
Christian Scientists' practice have questioned the integrity of
the individuals testifying to healings in the church's periodi-

cals. Some have questioned the reliability of details reported in the testimonies, since most, like the example just given, are by persons who are not medically trained.

Due weight needs to be given this caution. Even in diagnosed cases, testifiers are often reporting in their own words what physicians have said to them. The possibility that in some cases individuals have misinterpreted, misremembered, or otherwise inaccurately reported the remarks of doctors cannot be ruled out any more than the possibility in some cases of medical misdiagnosis.

On the other hand, a distinction is needed between legitimate questions of accuracy or comprehensiveness and the fixed position taken by some that these healings could not have happened and that therefore the testimonies must be mistaken. It is at least highly implausible to assume that all or even most of the healings reported in so large a body of testimonies can be attributed to such mistakes. In the case of coronary disease referred to above, a Boston cardiologist who reviewed the testifier's affidavit for the church found "certain obscurities" in the testifier's description but "no inconsistencies . . . except in the behavior of the doctor and/or in the patient's paraphrasing" and "no conflicts with medical doctrine except for the miracle of healing which is not in [doctors'] purview anyhow!" [11] Whatever the ultimate explanation for "miracles" of this sort, to assume *a priori* that they are impossible is to preclude serious medical or scientific inquiry into the phenomenon of spiritual healing.

The Christian Science church has not systematically collected medical records from testifiers. Historically, as one church official has written, its "focus has been on healing in the context of *worship*," [12] and while X-ray or other medical records have occasionally accompanied testimonies submitted to the church periodicals, the church has not required these of testifiers and has solicited them only rarely. For some testifiers, particularly those who have been through extremely difficult physical straits prior to a healing, "dredging up those memories" is itself a painful process and not something they wish to reinforce in the sharing of a significant spiritual victory.[13] In recent years hospital regulations governing release of medical records to past patients have become tighter and the obtaining of such records more costly.

The church does require each testifier to obtain verifying letters or statements from at least three other members who either witnessed the healing that is recounted or who are able to vouch more broadly for the integrity of the testifier. Some also include attesting statements by non-members, e.g., family members who are not Christian Scientists and occasionally even physicians, though the latter in general are predictably chary of appearing to give endorsement to a non-medical method of healing. One Phoenix, Arizona, physician who verified a healing of a shattered leg concluded his letter with the proviso that "No authority expressed or implied is given for publication of my verification or name...." [14] Even without such restrictions only a minority of the attestations are published—usually when they add substantive information to the testimony or when one or more of those attesting to a particular healing were directly involved in it.

Methodology.   This study involved the preparation of a database recording and categorizing the medical information contained in testimonies published in the denomination's periodicals from 1969–1988. Not included in this total is a scattering of healings related in religious articles but not specifically included in the testimony section of each issue. Though the database is limited to the latter, other healings related in the church's periodicals are subject to the same verification requirements as the testimonies and are also often medically significant—e.g., a healing of an adopted infant diagnosed as hydrocephalic and considered unable to develop normally. [15]

The database records the medical facts from each testimony in up to 21 discrete classifications or fields. These include the specific medical name of the condition healed, if given, or the generic nature of the condition, if not; the physical symptoms described in the testimony or other facts amplifying this description; the total duration of the condition; the length of time under Christian Science care; indication of medical diagnosis, if relevant, along with any factors elaborating the credibility or extensiveness of the diagnosis, such as hospital involvement, consultation with specialists, the involvement of multiple physicians, or taking of X-rays; any specific prognosis given or remarks made by physicians in the diagnostic process, including whether the condition was life-threatening and what the normal course of medical treatment would entail; and whether the healing was medically confirmed by after-the-fact examination. The database also distinguishes healings of children by age group and the decade in which the healing took place, when either piece of information is available.

While not excluding a margin of error in the recording of this data, the database fields have been defined narrowly to minimize misinterpretation of either the testifier's language or the medical facts. Cases listed as medically diagnosed, for example, include only those where a diagnosis was specifically mentioned in or reasonably indicated by the testimony. This excludes the large number of similar cases where the wording of the testimony strongly implies that there was medical diagnosis but does not provide sufficient information to make it clear. It also excludes cases in which healings might be partially attributable to prior medical treatment or in which the diagnoses might be considered especially tenuous (such as a diabetes case in which a patient tested positive for the disease one day and negative the next, after specific prayer in Christian Science and despite the doctor's insistence that the first test had been accurate[16]).

Similar commonsense cautions increase the integrity of the rest of the database. Hospitals, specialists or X-rays are noted only where they are mentioned explicitly—again, leaving out many other cases where the conditions healed were almost certainly diagnosed in hospitals by specialists and/or with X-rays but where the testimony does not go into these details. Healings of substance abuse problems and self-imposed addictions (in one case a twenty-year heroin habit[17]) are not listed, but healings of specific physiological damage from addictions or substance abuse (such as cirrhosis of the liver[18]) are. A condition is listed as life-threatening only if the testimony states explicitly that a physician involved in the diagnosis said it was. Testimonies that do not mention a physician's statement to that effect are not included in this category even when the healings involve diseases normally considered life-threatening, such as leukemia.

Findings. Since there is no standard format for the testimonies, relatively few provide comprehensive medical information covering all fields in the database. Nevertheless, the substantial information collectible from these sources makes clear that healing in Christian Science is by no means limited to psychosomatic conditions or to cases involving self- or otherwise "unsubstantiated" diagnoses, as has often been assumed.[19]

The vast majority (over 80%) of the 7,154 testimonies published from 1969–1988 include healings of bodily disorders. The high percentage of testimonies including physical healing illustrates its continuing importance among contemporary Christian Scientists, though as Stephen Gottschalk notes, their use of the term healing extends to difficulties of all kinds.[20] Single testimonies often refer to healings of both bodily illness and other problems. This particular group of testimonies includes, for example, healings of marital discords, business problems, alcoholism, effects of sexual abuse or family tragedy, suicidal depression, nervous breakdown, religious despair, immoral or destructive patterns of behavior, and incidents of protection in war.

The total number of physical healings recounted in this period is over 10,000. Of these some 2,337 involve healings of medically diagnosed conditions. The latter figure is limited to healings related firsthand by the individual healed or, in the case of healings of children, by a parent. It does not count numerous healings of medically diagnosed conditions which are related secondhand—e.g., an Iowa woman's vivid account of her father's healing in minutes of an eye injured in an accident and diagnosed as permanently blinded[21]—unless they are accompanied by a published firsthand confirming statement. Testimonies by second-, third-, or fourth-generation church members frequently refer to significant earlier healings experienced by parents or grandparents, but these are also excluded from the statistical totals unless otherwise documented.

Among the medically diagnosed cases, 285 made reference

to specialists, 284 to X-rays, 453 to the involvement of more than one physician, 507 to the involvement of a hospital in the diagnosis. The medical contacts in these cases essentially involved diagnosis alone or else tangibly unsuccessful medical treatment, sometimes for an extended period, prior to the testifier's decision to turn to Christian Science for healing. In 623 cases healings were medically confirmed by follow-up examinations. In 222 cases ranging from extreme trauma caused by auto collisions to serious degenerative diseases, the testifiers referred specifically to terminal or life-threatening prognoses by physicians. In some of these cases the testifier's survival many years after such a prognosis corroborates the healing more fully than a follow-up examination could.

The list of diagnosed conditions healed covers an extremely broad range of injuries, disorders, and diseases: at least 27 healings of malignancy or cancer (including bone cancer, lymph cancer, skin cancer, cancer of the liver, breast, intestine, and uterus), 42 of tumor, 16 of polio, 68 of tuberculosis, 38 of pneumonia (seven of double pneumonia, two with collapsed lung), at least 88 of heart disorders, 23 of kidney disorders (two of Bright's disease), 203 of broken bones (further analysis below), 71 of childbirth complications (such as uremic poisoning, four still births), nine of meningitis, 24 of appendicitis (eight acute), 16 of scarlet fever, 16 of rheumatic fever, 11 of cataract, 12 of diabetes (one as complication of pregnancy, one juvenile case), 13 of pernicious anemia, 12 of rheumatoid or degenerative arthritis, two of gangrene, three of glaucoma, seven of hepatitis, three of leukemia, six of multiple sclerosis, seven of blindness (48 of other vision deficiencies such as astigmatism or nearsightedness), 13 of goiter, eight of curvature of the spine, 13 of epilepsy, three of crossed eyes, one of cleft palate.

Even this partial accounting belies the contention that all or most of the conditions healed in Christian Science are self-limiting and "would have gone away by themselves." But the mere listing of conditions healed in itself gives no indication of the more compelling circumstances related in many of the testimonies—the large number, for instance, in which conditions persisted under medical treatment but were quickly and decisively healed in Christian Science (as when a testifier was

healed within two days of severe allergic reactions which had
been lifelong and a longstanding unrelated knee injury[22]).
There are also many in which damage to the affected organ
was deemed irreparable (as in at least one of the healings of
blindness, where the iris and pupil in both eyes had been severely injured[23]) or in which physicians themselves termed the
healings miraculous (as when an elderly testifier was healed of
nerve damage which had been diagnosed as incurable and rendered her immobile[24]).

In still other cases, the actual course of the healings described makes traditional explanatory labels such as natural
"remission" virtually meaningless. In one Australian's healing
of multiple sclerosis, the testifier turned to Christian Science
after his condition had steadily degenerated over a period of
two-and-a-half years. He was completely paralyzed, nearly
blind, could not speak or feed himself, and one leg had become
shorter than the other. His condition stabilized immediately
under prayer in Christian Science and within several weeks
began to improve gradually but steadily. He was cared for in a
home for Christian Scientists needing special nursing help. In
eight months he was able to walk and not long thereafter relin-
quished the invalid pension he had been receiving.[25]

The full list of diagnosed conditions healed includes virtually all classes of disease—infectious, congenital, immuno-
logical, neurological, etc. It includes conditions regarded
as biologically-caused as well as conditions considered
emotionally-generated. It also includes healings of medically
incurable as well as medically treatable conditions. These
healings do not fit what a physician writing in *The New England Journal of Medicine* called a "mechanistic and reductionis-
tic" model of health,[26] but as a church official has written, they
"constitute evidence that can and should be taken seriously by
rational people . . . If the evidence doesn't fit the model, the
need is to reexamine the model, not arbitrarily deny the
evidence!"[27] Healings of medically diagnosed conditions represent only a fraction of the healings shared in the testimonies,
but they provide a useful point of departure for objective
study.

Healings of children. Gratitude for healings of children is a major theme in Christian Science testimonies. Testifiers often refer to their own healings *as* children in Christian Science families as well as to healings of their children. Typically the choice of Christian Science healing for their children is rooted in such personal experiences. In some instances—one of the meningitis cases, for example[28]—testifiers describe turning to Christian Science in desperation for their children when medical aid has been unsuccessful.

The 20 years of testimonies under study included 2,451 healings of children, 640 of which involved conditions that were medically diagnosed. Many of these testimonies do not indicate the age of the child healed, but of those that do, 801 involved small children under six, 394 youngsters between six and twelve, and 319 teenagers under eighteen. The proportion of testimonies indicating diagnosis by specialists, in a hospital, or by more than one physician is similar to that for adults.

In at least 88 cases the examining doctor pronounced a child's illness life-threatening. Many of these healings involved small children—at least three of the spinal meningitis cases (one in which a pediatrician provided a verifying statement for reference but not for publication[29]), five of pneumonia or double pneumonia, one of food poisoning, one of diphtheria, one of wet lung, one of brain fever and chorea, two of heart disorders (one of fibroelastosis), one of stomach obstruction. In another case—a recovery described as a miracle after a drowning accident involving a two-year-old—a Quaker physician provided a verifying statement for publication.[30] An older child was healed of mitral valve lesion, despite a prognosis of permanent invalidism if the child survived.[31] Two healings of ruptured appendix involved teenagers.

Other medically diagnosed conditions healed in children's cases included, in addition to numerous of the conditions listed earlier, defective glands, loss of eyesight from chemical burns, pleurisy, stomach tumor, bowed legs (a premature newborn also suffering from a serious case of jaundice[32]), bone disease (a boy of eight healed in five days after a medical prognosis of impairment for many months and possible permanent disability[33]), eight of foot deformities (at least two of clubbed feet), seven of hernia (including double hernia and umbilical hernia), 13 of asthma (one life-threatening case), hypogamma-globulinemia (an autoimmune deficiency), seven of hearing loss or impairment, at least five of convulsions, at least six of mastoiditis.

Perhaps the most unusual of these testimonies concern healings effected by the children themselves. Christian Scientists do not consider prayer exclusive to adults or healing beyond the spiritual capacities of children. The denomination's periodicals include occasional testimonies by children, and in religious terms the tradition emphasizes the natural responsiveness of even small children to God.[34] One California man, now a parent himself, told of a healing of collapsed lung through his own prayer as an eight year old. At the time he attended the Christian Science Sunday School but his parents were not practicing Christian Scientists. His healing, which occurred at the hospital on the night before a scheduled operation, initially met with disbelief on the part of both surgeon and parents but was confirmed by before-and-after X-rays.[35]

Broken bones. For several reasons, testimonies relating to the healing of broken bones provide a unique medical window both on Christian Scientists' experience and on what might be called the physiological effects of prayer. Since no medication is involved in the setting of broken bones, Christian Scientists sometimes employ a physician for this purpose—one of the few circumstances in which a Christian Science practitioner may be employed simultaneously with a physician on the same case. As a result of this interface, there is an unusually large number of cases in which healings of serious breaks or fractures have been confirmed by medical evidence. Because X-ray diagnosis of broken bones has for many decades been relatively straightforward and reliable, this study surveyed testimonies on these particular healings over an extended period of forty years from 1949 to 1988.

The testimonies published during these decades included some 599 healings of broken bones. Of these, 273 indicated definitive medical diagnosis or confirmation of the break, 245 specified X-rays. As in previous sections, the diagnosed cases do not include those in which the wording merely implied diagnosis but did not indicate it clearly. Nor do they include cases where a physician offered an unconfirmed visual diagnosis at the scene of an accident (as when, after an equestrian accident, a doctor present advised one teenager she had a probable broken hip[36]).

Among undiagnosed or self-diagnosed cases, a minority involved such "probable" or "possible" breaks. More, however, involved physical evidence that was clear and unambiguous. Many of the most striking are cases in which full healing took place within hours or days wholly without contact with physicians. In one incident a South African teenager whose arm had been broken the previous day in a sporting match—a break confirmed by the team trainer and involving a protruding bone—felt the bone move into place within ten minutes after calling for specific help in Christian Science and had no further trouble with the arm.[37] In another a Canadian woman was walking and "carry[ing] heavy groceries" two days after breaking her ankle in a fall that left a bone sticking out "across both sides of the foot." She, too, felt the bone move into place and said it was "all [she] could do" to walk rather than "run and leap and praise God" like the lame man healed in the New Testament book of Acts.[38]

Medically diagnosed cases also include numerous similar healings, though not all include a specific chronology. Many refer to healings as "quick" or "gradual" but do not provide sufficient information to determine recovery times with assurance. Of those diagnosed cases where such information is provided, 91 involved healings which were complete in three weeks or less. In at least 11 of these cases the healing took one day or less. In another 43 cases the healing took from two days to a week. In another 24 cases the healing took between one and two weeks. These figures do not include cases where the testifier spoke only of the bone being "set" within a certain number of days but did not clarify the time taken for full recovery.

Cases healed within one day included, among others, a fractured jaw, confirmed in writing by a dentist whose diagnosis was made in consultation with a physician;[39] a broken wrist, where one X-ray confirmed the break and a second X-ray several hours later showed no break;[40] three crushed vertebrae from a motorcycle accident, verified as healed the next day by X-rays taken at an orthopedic hospital (where examining physicians stated that the injury appeared to have been healing for months);[41] and two of severely shattered noses healed while the testifiers waited in a hospital emergency room between first and second X-rays.[42]

Cases healed within one week included an arm broken in several places, set through prayer within hours (again between the first and second set of X-rays) and completely healed in five days;[43] a broken bone and cartilage in the leg, where the attending physician indicated that the patient might have a permanent limp or lameness even with surgery;[44] and a broken shoulder blade which was threatening to puncture a lung, healed in three days before a scheduled operation in a military hospital.[45] One case healed in just over a week involved a teenager with a severely fractured pelvis after an automobile accident. (The medical prognosis had been for at least a two-month convalescence.)[46]

This highly abbreviated sampling does not convey the many unusual features of those cases in which full recovery was more gradual. Even in these the testimonies routinely refer to healings accomplished far more quickly than the attending physicians expected as well as to the perfect setting of even complicated breaks through prayer. Many involve rapid healings of persons of advanced age. In many cases casts or surgical procedures were found unnecessary because of progress evident by the time a physician was consulted. In others specific medical prognoses for permanent disability—e.g., that patients would never walk again or would never regain full use of limbs—were overcome.

At least 29 of these testimonies refer to injuries described by physicians as life-threatening. One Michigan case in this category involved broken vertebrae, broken ribs, a crushed left shoulder, a fractured skull and severe internal hemorrhaging after a nine-foot fall to a terrazzo floor. No taping or casts were used because the testifier was not expected to survive. By the sixth day after the accident she was able to walk to a chair, by the third week she attended church and resumed household duties, by the fourth she resumed all normal activities. The physician on the case acknowledged that a "higher power" was responsible for the healing and told the testifier to "stick with" Christian Science.[47] While statements such as this represent only subjective opinion even when coming from a physician, the large body of testimony on healings of broken bones, taken as a whole, provides significant further evidence of healing effects not readily attributable to the body's normal recuperative processes.

Limits and conclusions. Christian Scientists' most controversial premise is less that exceptional healings happen through prayer than that they are not exceptional—that spiritual healing can be relied on systematically with favorable results.

This study addresses that issue only indirectly. It does not provide comparative cure or mortality rates, nor does it consider cases in which healing prayer has not been effective. The evidence accumulated in the testimonies suggests that there may be no truly "incurable" conditions, but there are obviously cases that are not cured. Christian Scientists attribute these neither to divine will nor to personal guilt, but see consistent effectiveness in spiritual healing as requiring a high level of dedication and above all love. In that respect it resembles the best of medical practice. It is not possible from available information to determine whether the proportion of such cases in Christian Science is lower or higher than the proportion of such cases under medical care. The practical, logistical—and, frankly, spiritual and ethical—difficulties of conducting controlled experimental studies on Christian Scientists' practice would appear almost insurmountable.

On the other hand, the evidence that is available strongly supports the contention that healing in Christian Scientists' experience has been real, frequent, and often not explainable under ordinary medical rubrics. At the very least, it provides substantial objective grounds for taking the phenomenon of spiritual healing seriously—even, as one commentator on medical ethics has written, "those with reflexive skepticism on the subject." [48] A great deal of medical research is based on individual case data rather than controlled studies. Christian Scientists argue that these particular cases have far-reaching implications for both religion and medicine, but irrespective of any theological position, the facts themselves are significant and cannot be scientifically disregarded. Christian Scientists' consistent choice of spiritual healing is understandable only in light of these facts.

[1] O'Toole, K. "Researcher says prayer is good for your health." *San Francisco Examiner*, January 24, 1989: A-2.

[2] "Religion in Healing." *Southern Medical Journal*, July 7, 1988; 81:819–820.

[3] Cf. England, R.W. "Some Aspects of Christian Science as Reflected in Letters of Testimony." *American Journal of Sociology*, March 1954; LIX:448–453. Reply by Davis, Will B. *American Journal of Sociology*, September 1954; LX:184–5.

[4] Testifier's correspondence: Church files. See *The Christian Science Journal*, October 1986; 104:628–629.

[5] San Francisco; Harper & Row, 149.

[6] Phinney, A.W. "Healing and the Nature of God." *The Christian Science Journal*, April 1989; 107:27.

[7] Quoted in Boston, Robert, "Prescription for Controversy: The Courts and Christian Science." *Church & State*, March 1989:10.

[8] *Christian Science Sentinel*, April 10, 1978; 80:587.

[9] Peel, Robert. *Spiritual Healing in a Scientific Age*:69–73.

[10] Temple University Hospital: Unit history. Simpson, Teressa 10/3/68–10/22/68.

[11] Comments of Dr. Richard A. Bloomfield, July 15, 1982: Church files.

[12] Correspondence: Nathan Talbot to Dr. Arthur Caplan (Center for Bioethics, University of Minnesota), August 24, 1988: Church files.

[13] Testifier's correspondence: Church files.

[14] "To whom it may concern," February 15, 1979: Church files. See *Christian Science Sentinel*, March 17, 1980; 82:466–468.

[15] Interview, "What it takes to care": *Christian Science Sentinel*, September 19, 1988; 90:12–16.

[16] *Christian Science Sentinel*, October 18, 1982; 84:1800–1802.

[17] *Christian Science Sentinel*, September 20, 1982; 84:1626–1628.

[18] *Christian Science Sentinel*, October 9, 1978; 80:1678–1680.

[19] Boston, Robert. "Prescription for Controversy," *op cit*:10.

[20] Gottschalk, Stephen. *The Emergence of Christian Science in American Religious Life*. Berkeley: University of California Press, 1973:222.

[21] *Christian Science Sentinel*, January 5, 1974; 76:31–32.

[22] *The Christian Science Journal*, June 1985; 103:395–396.

[23] *The Christian Science Journal*, October 1986; 104:628–629.

[24] *Christian Science Sentinel*, October 24, 1983; 85:1842–1844.

[25] *The Christian Science Journal*, March 1987; 105:48–50.

[26] Ross, Ira. "The Paradox of Health." *The New England Journal of Medicine*, August 11, 1988; 319:378.

[27] Correspondence: Nathan Talbot to Dr. Arthur Caplan, *op cit.*

[28] *Christian Science Sentinel*, November 18, 1985; 87:1988–1990.

[29] *Christian Science Sentinel*, May 11, 1987; 89:29–30.

[30] *Christian Science Sentinel*, October 24, 1988; 90:30–32.

[31] *Christian Science Sentinel*, December 27, 1982; 84:2220–2221.

[32] *The Christian Science Journal*, April 1985; 103:264–266.

[33] *Christian Science Sentinel*, July 18, 1988; 90:41–42.

[34] Peel, Robert. "The Christian Science Practitioner." *Journal of Pastoral Counseling*, Spring 1969; IV:1:42.

[35] *Christian Science Sentinel*, September 22, 1986; 88:1773–1774.

[36] *The Christian Science Journal*, June 1980; 98:331.

[37] *Christian Science Sentinel*, October 29, 1966; 68:1919–1920.

[38] *The Christian Science Journal*, March 1972; 90:162–163.

[39] *The Christian Science Journal*, September 1965; 83:613–614.

[40] *The Christian Science Journal*, September 1981; 99:543–544.

[41] *Christian Science Sentinel*, May 21, 1984; 86:895–897.

[42] *The Christian Science Journal*, April 1964; 82:223–224. *Christian Science Sentinel*, May 25, 1987; 89:33–34.

[43] *Christian Science Sentinel*, June 19, 1976; 78:1096–1097.

[44] *Christian Science Sentinel*, September 18, 1976; 78:1635–1636.

[45] *Christian Science Sentinel*, April 24, 1965; 67:729–731.

[46] *Christian Science Sentinel*, June 26, 1965; 67:1124–1125.

[47] *Christian Science Sentinel*, August 7, 1965; 67:1392–1394.

[48] Wind, James P. "Does Faith Make a Difference?" *Second Opinion*, March 1988; 7:8–9.